Your opinion is our greatest gift!
If you have enjoyed this coloring book, we would greatly appreciate it if you could leave a review in Amazon. Help us inspire others through therapeutic coloring.

COLORTHERAPY ART.

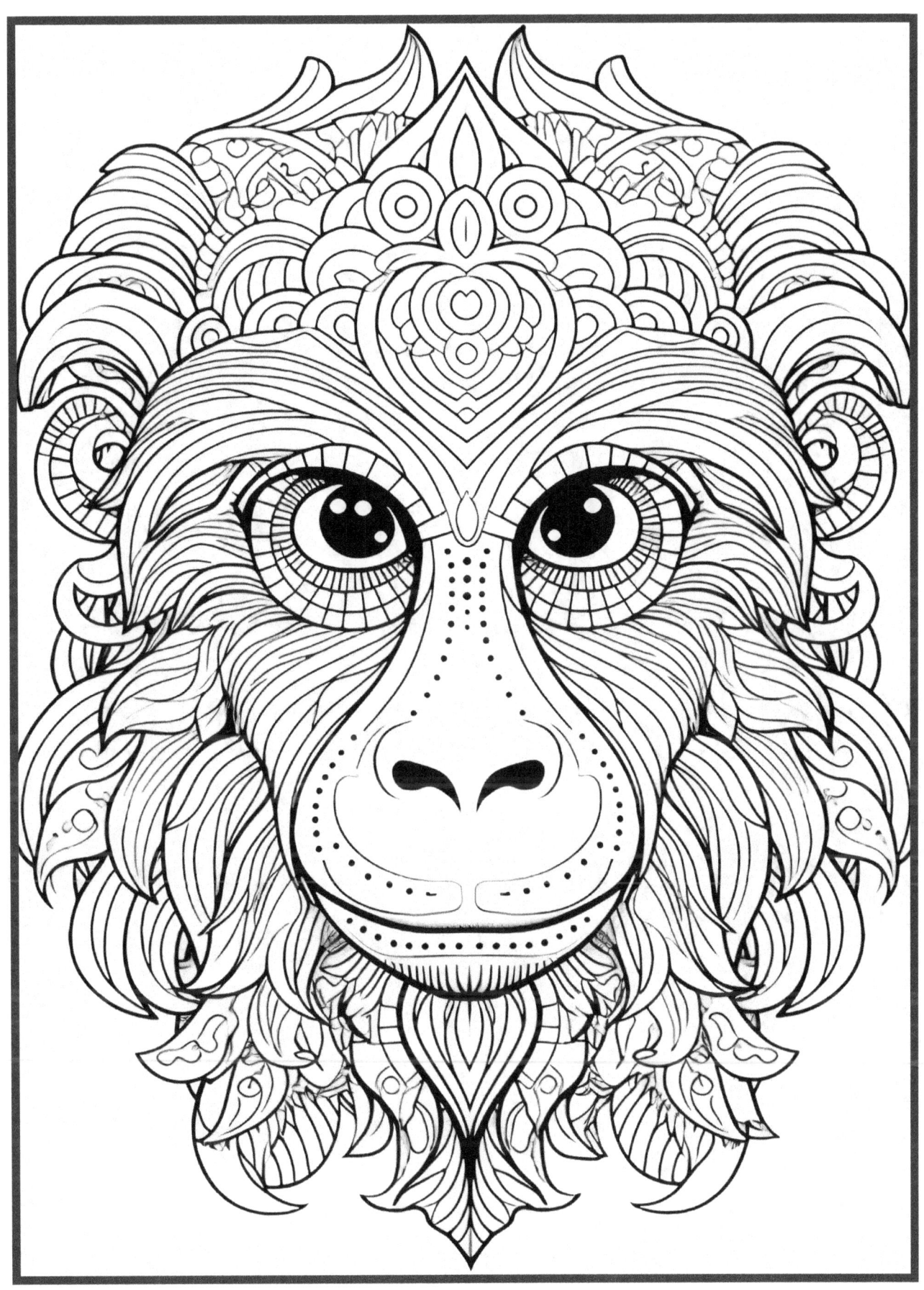

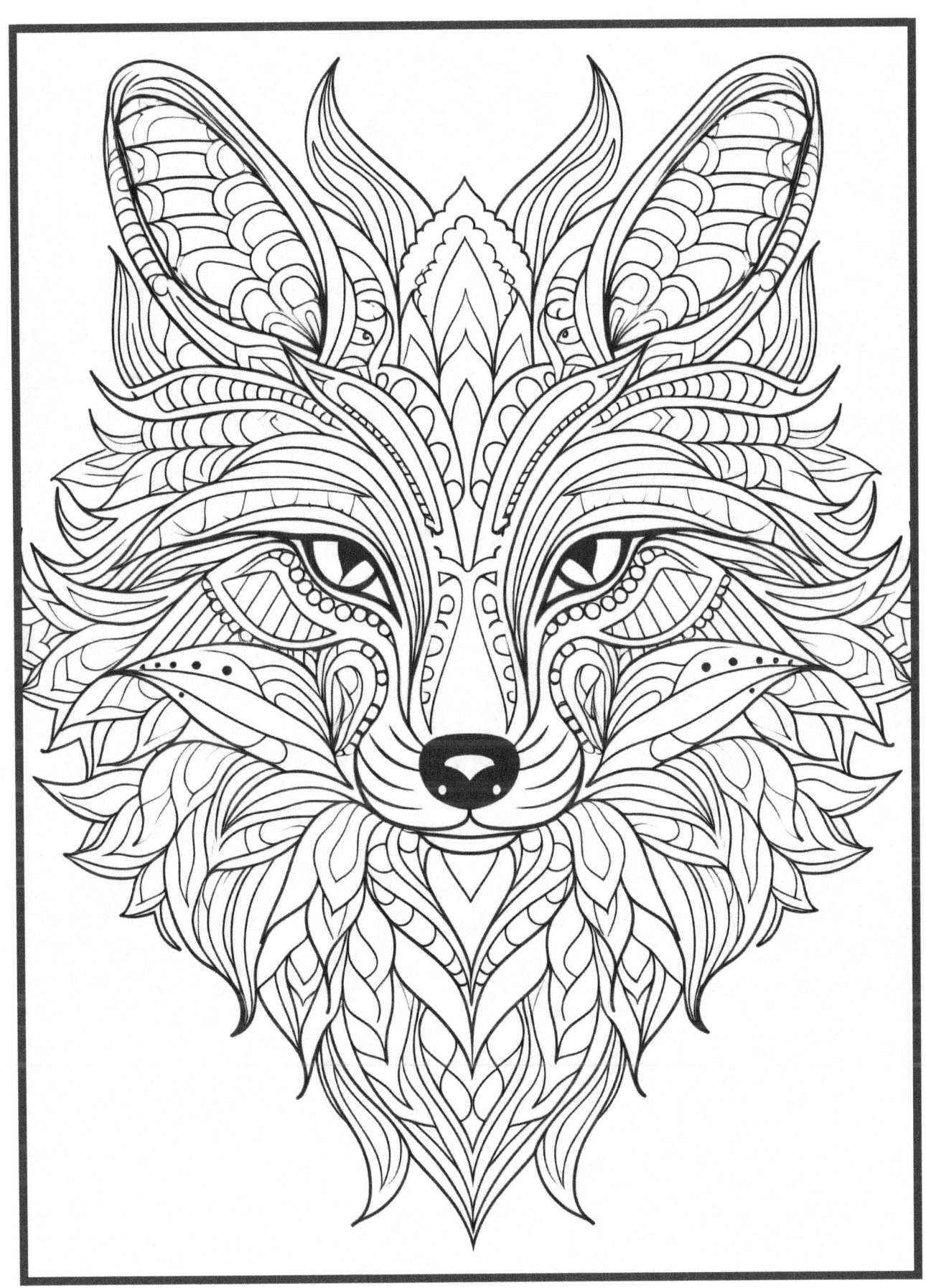

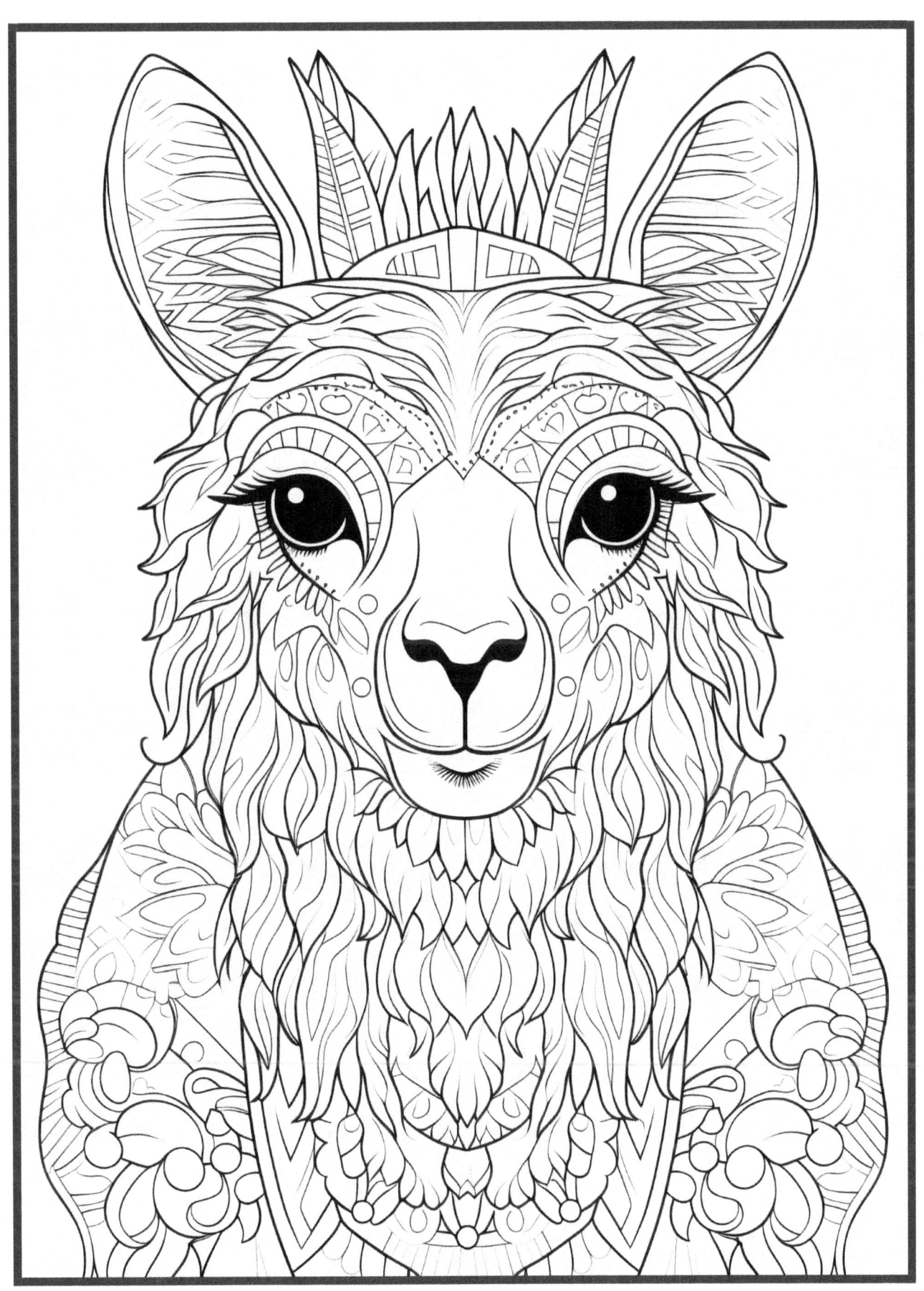

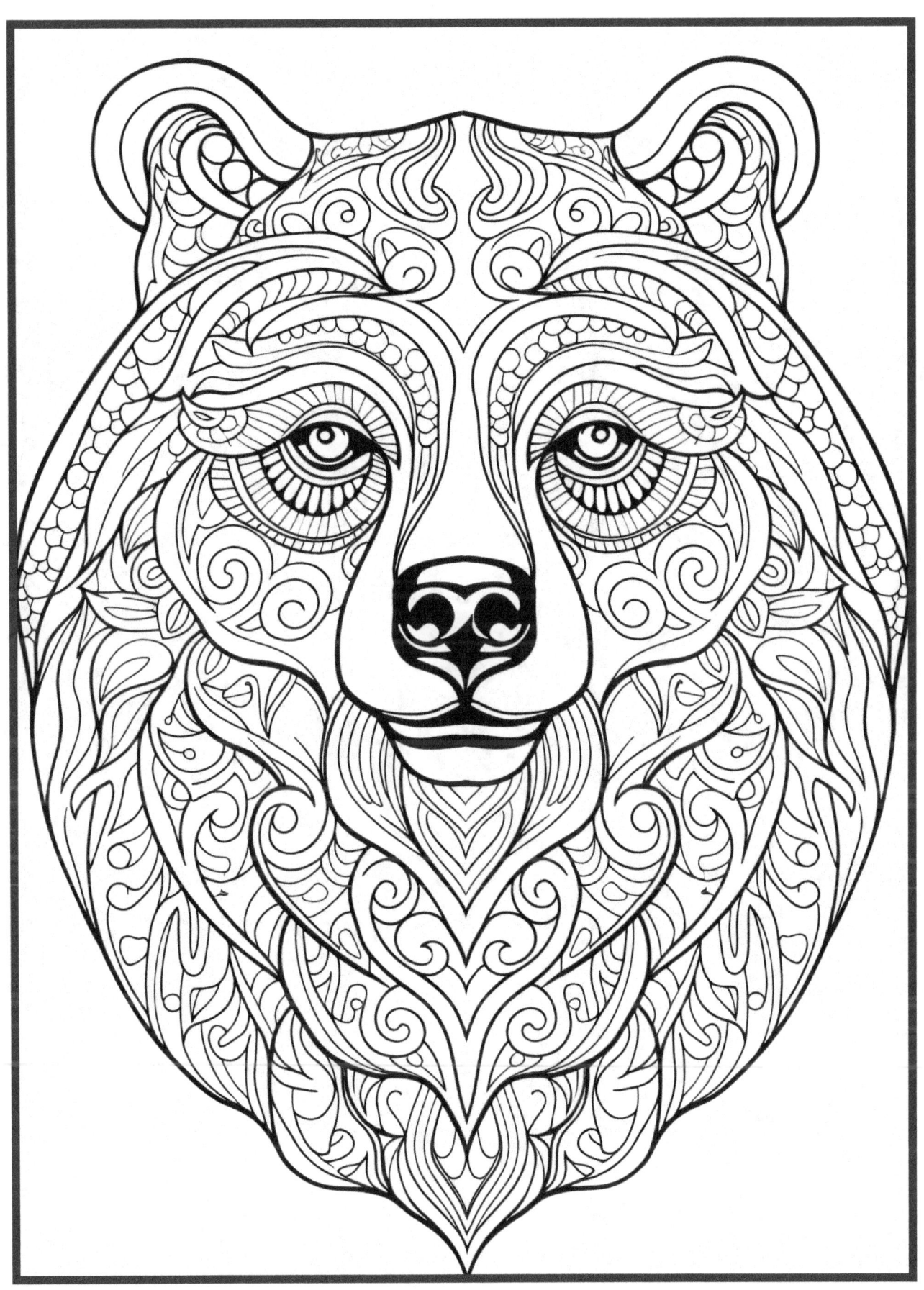

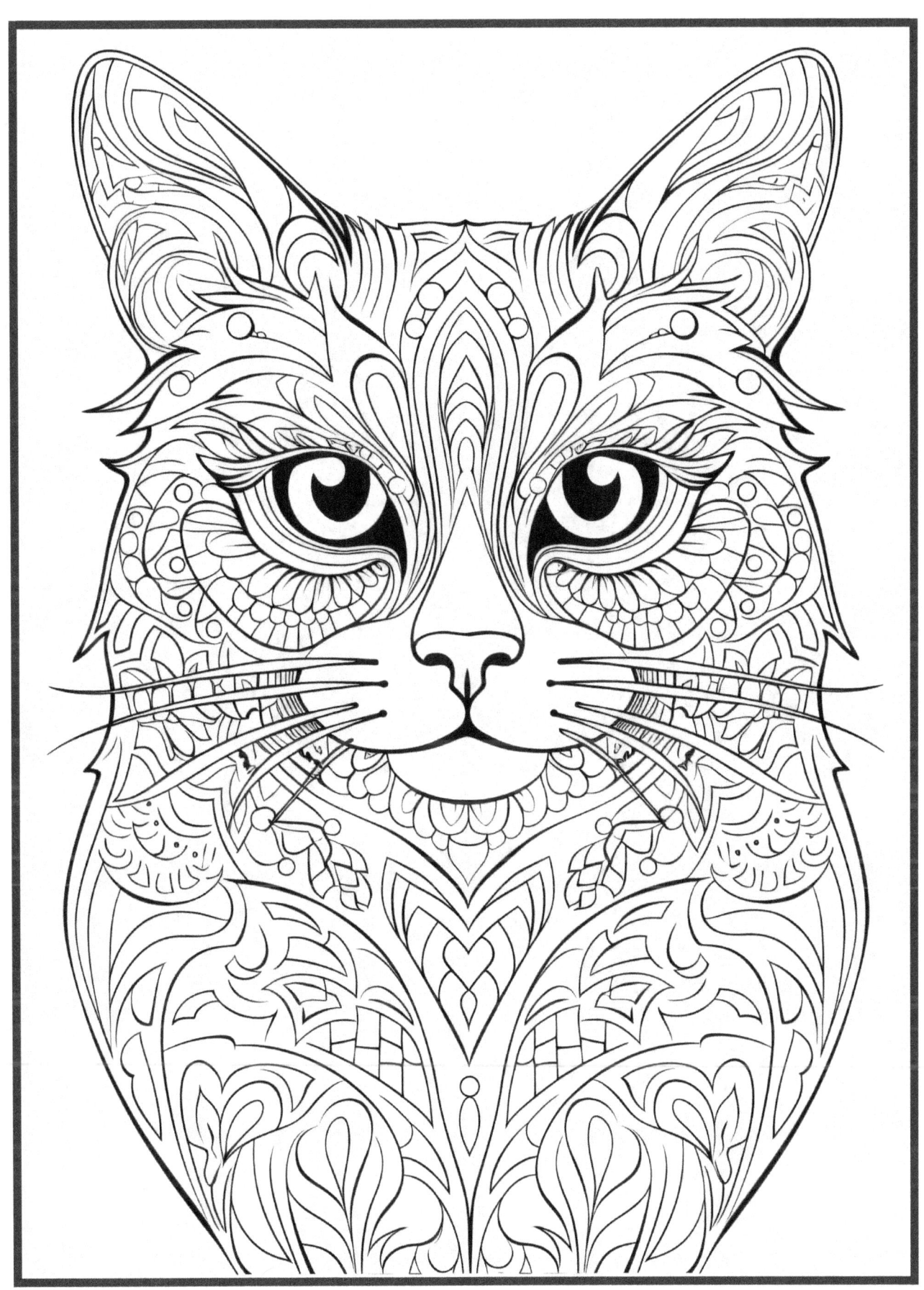

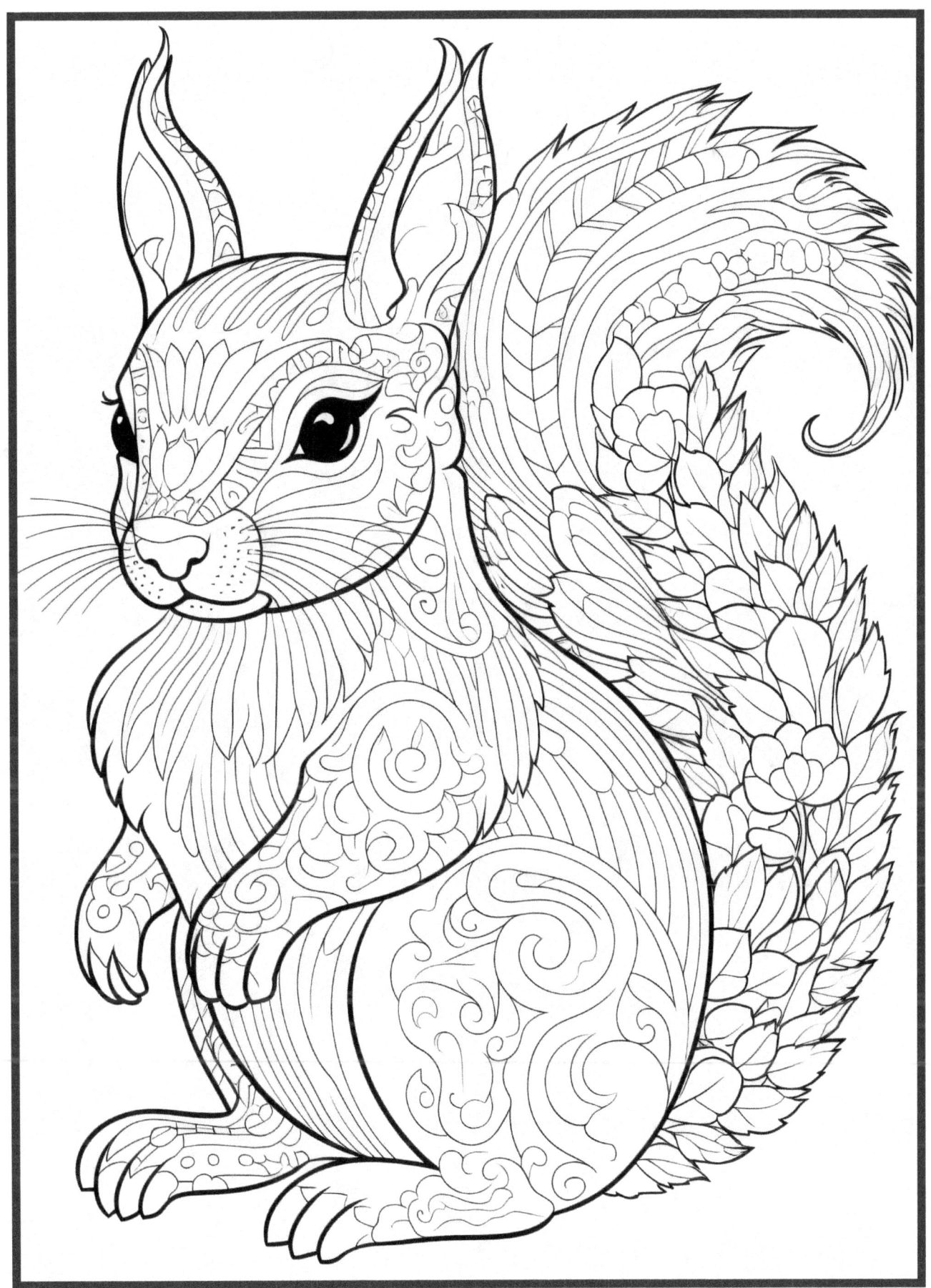

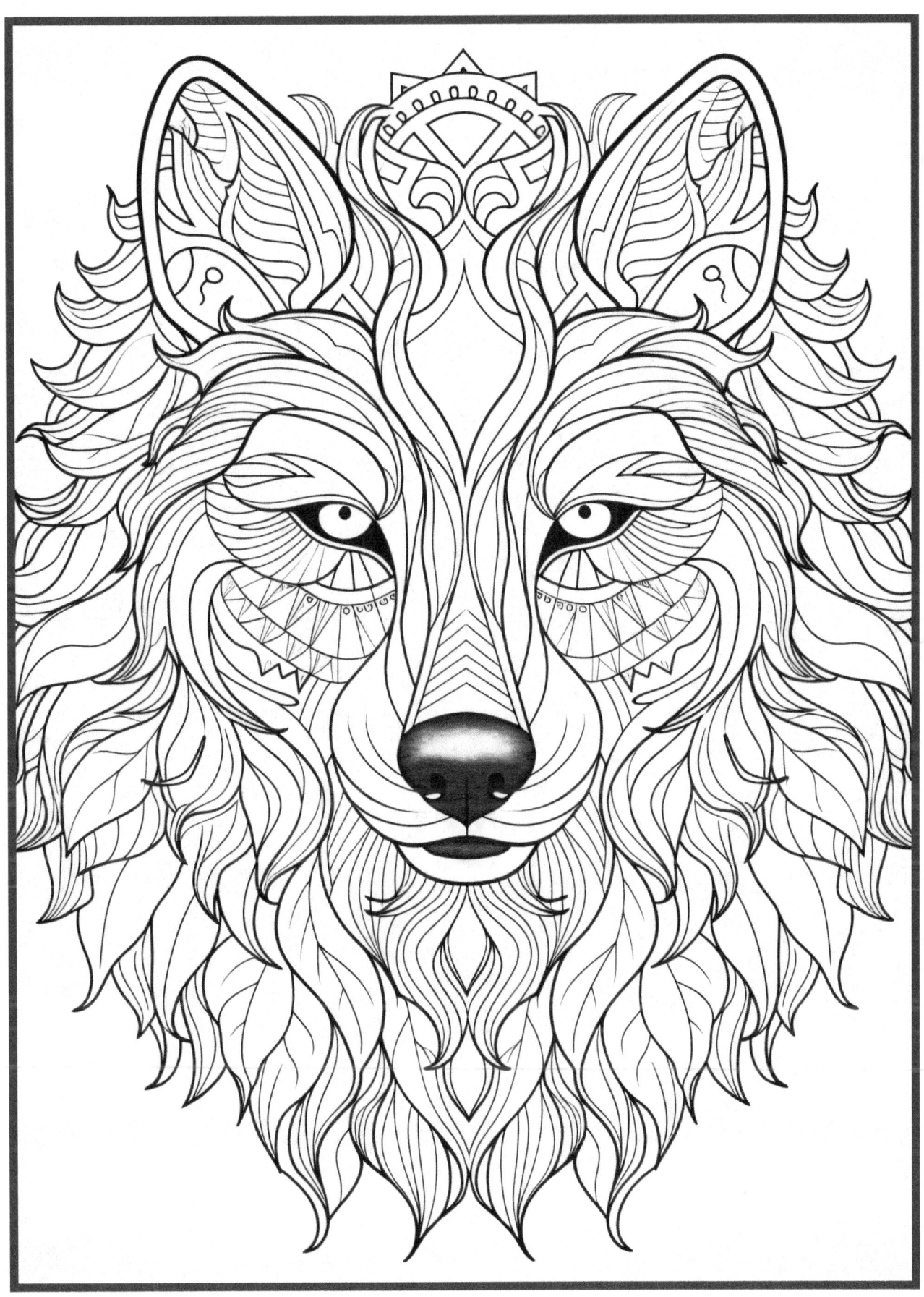

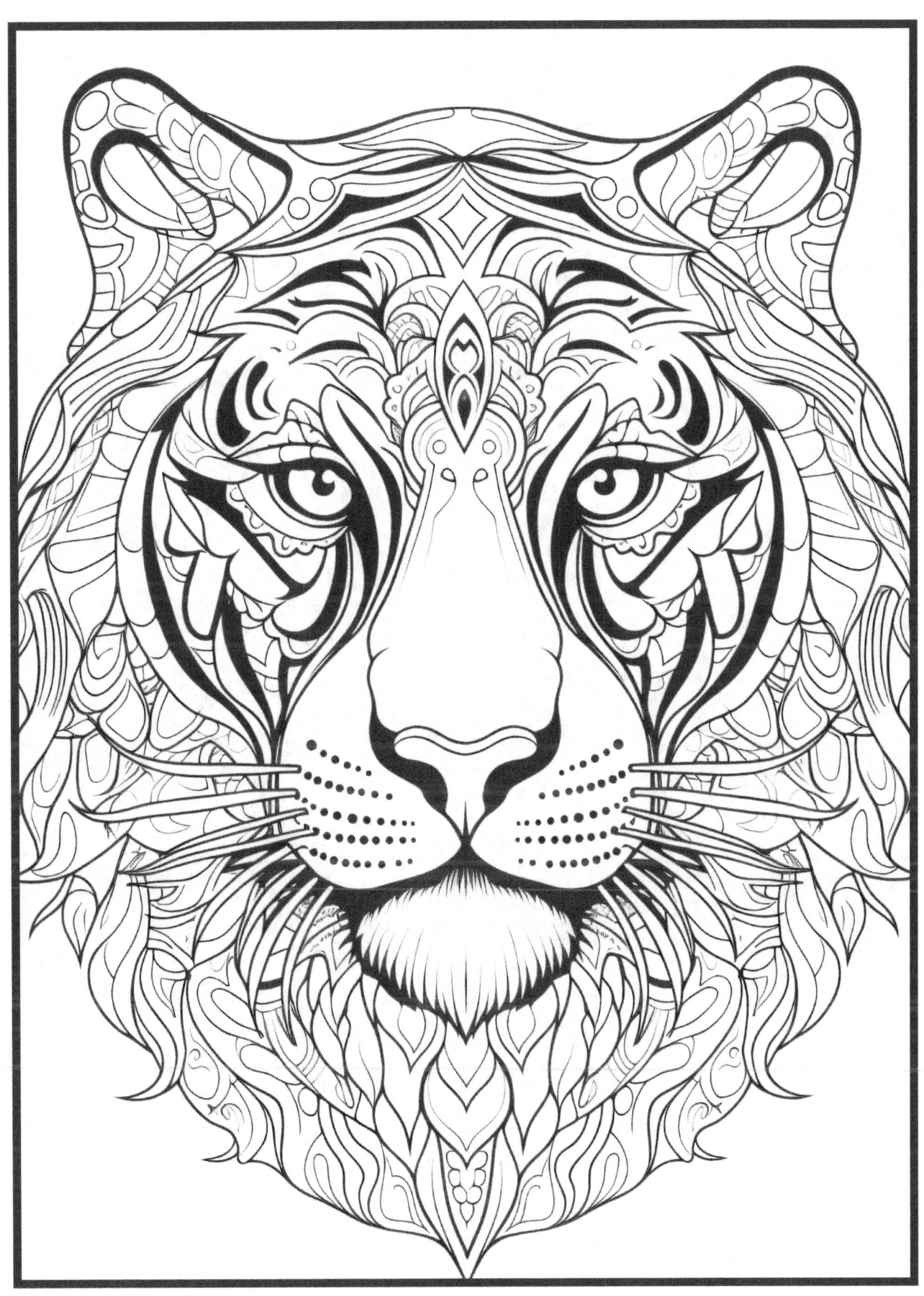

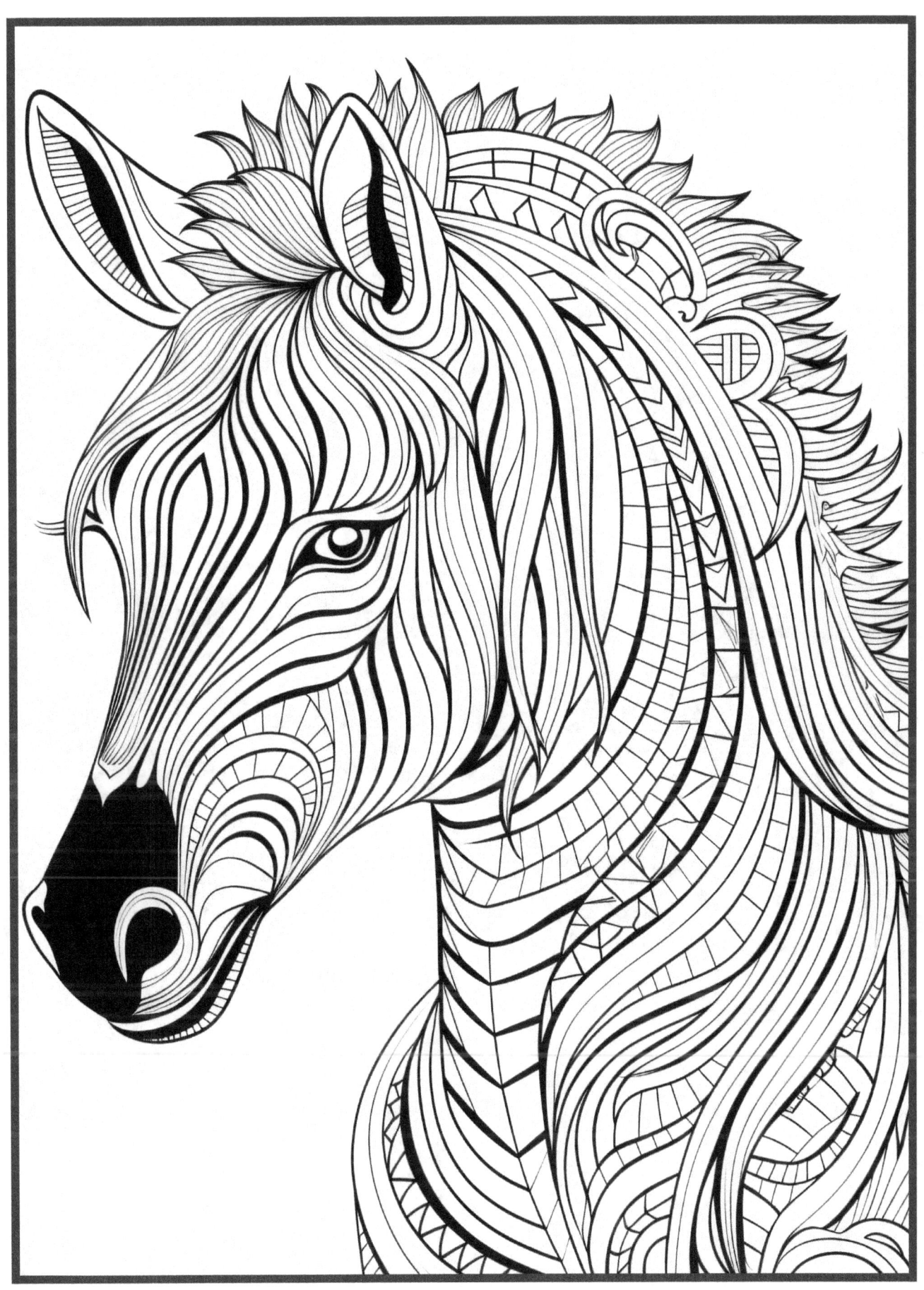

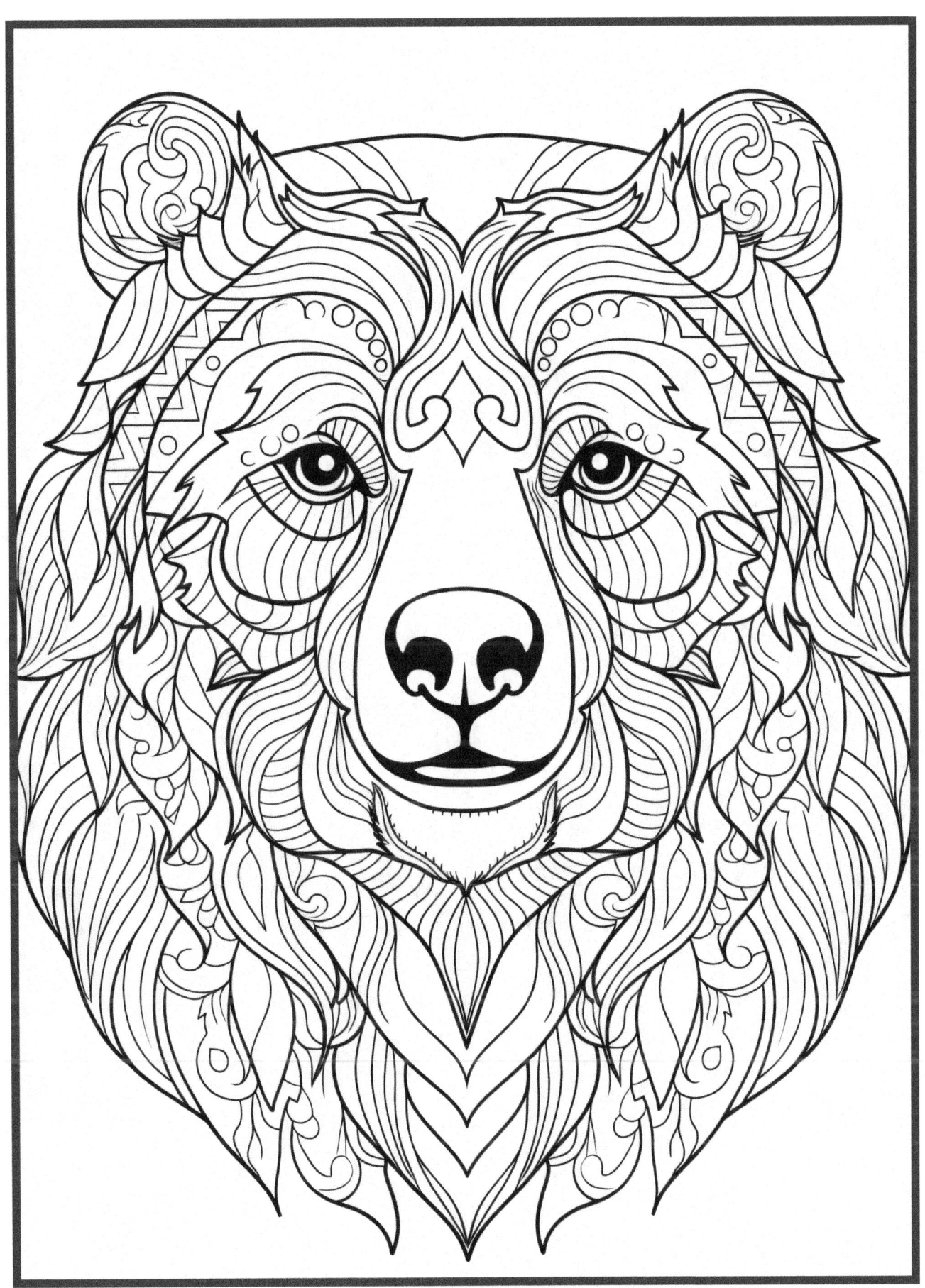

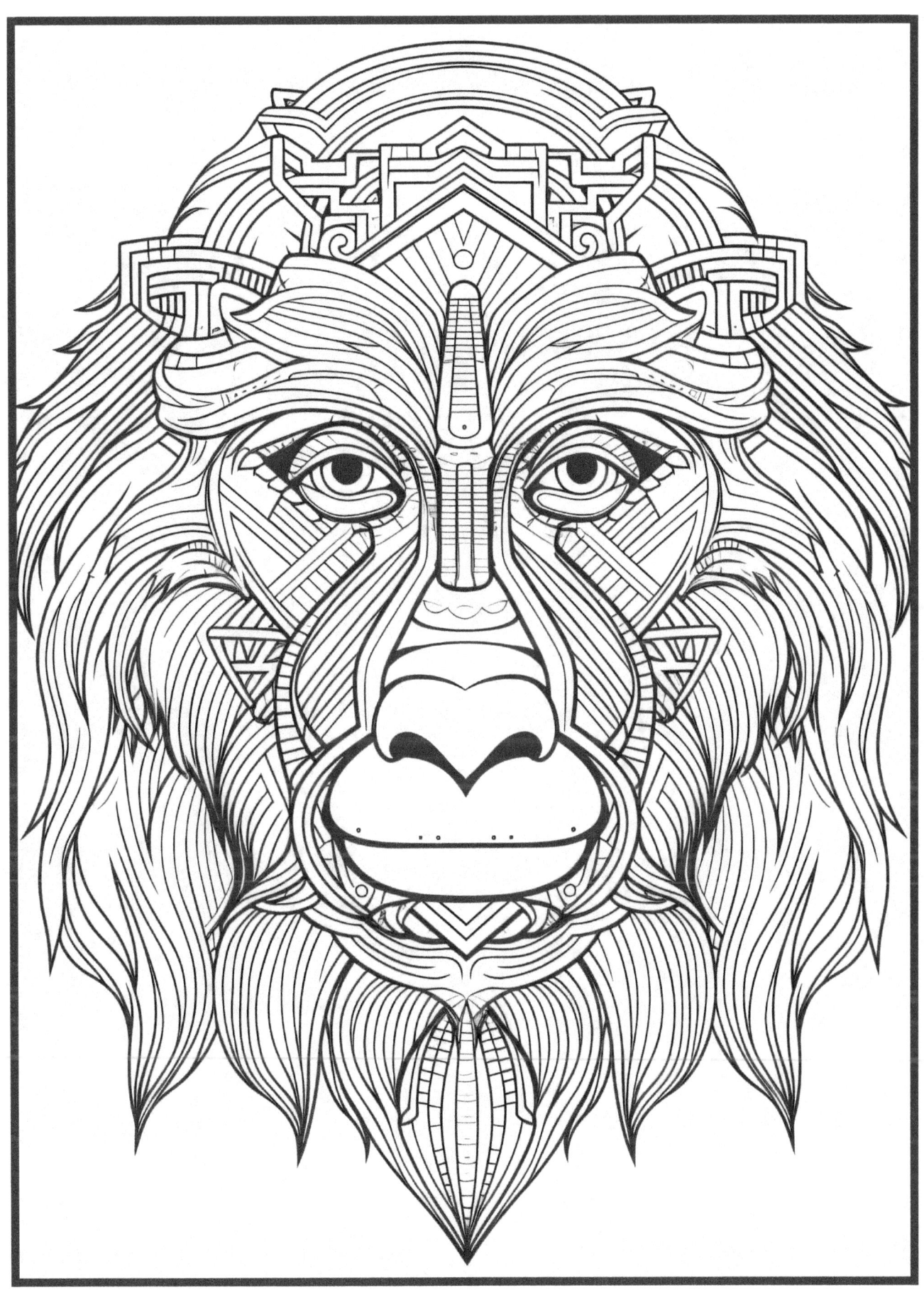

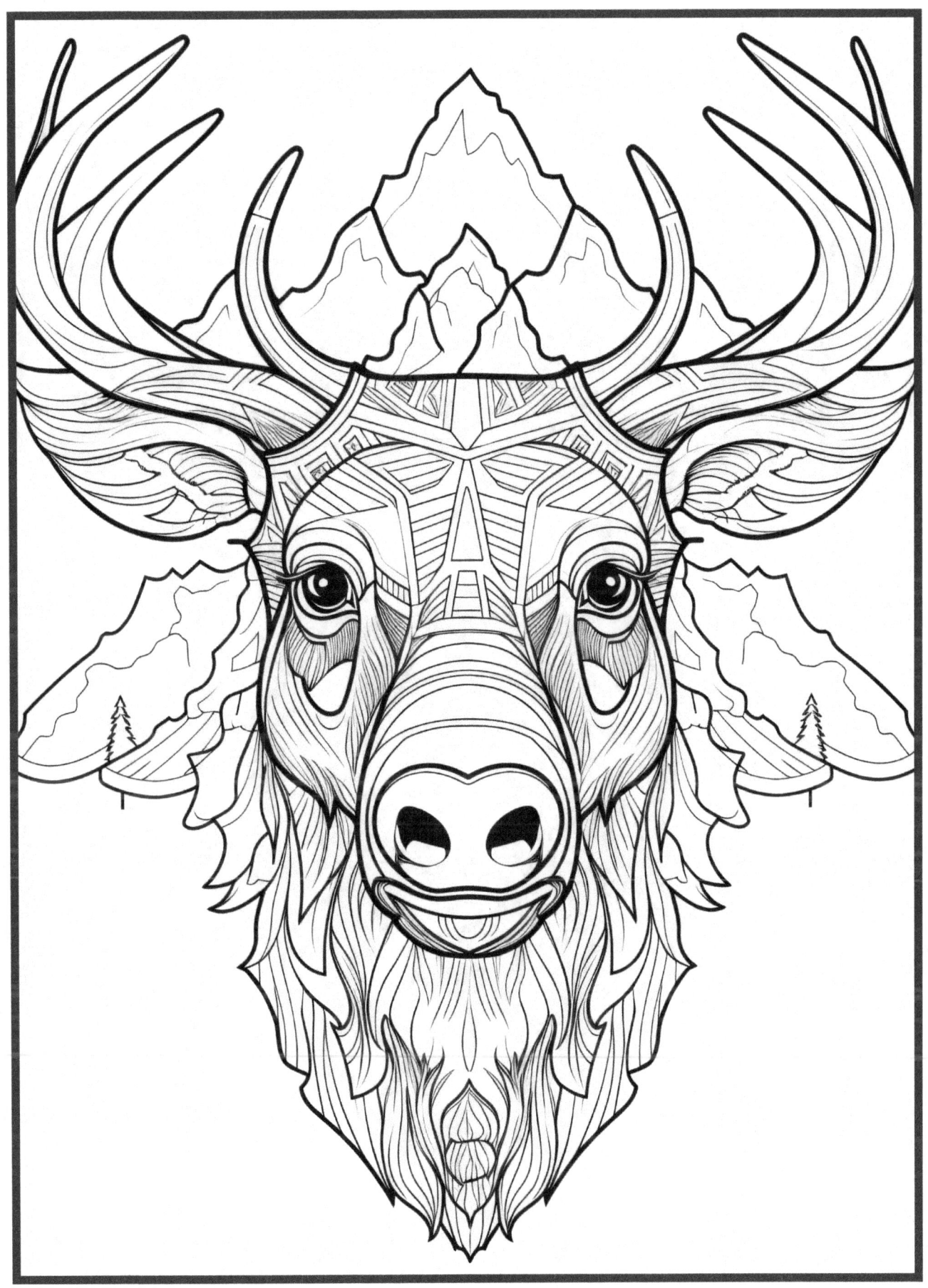

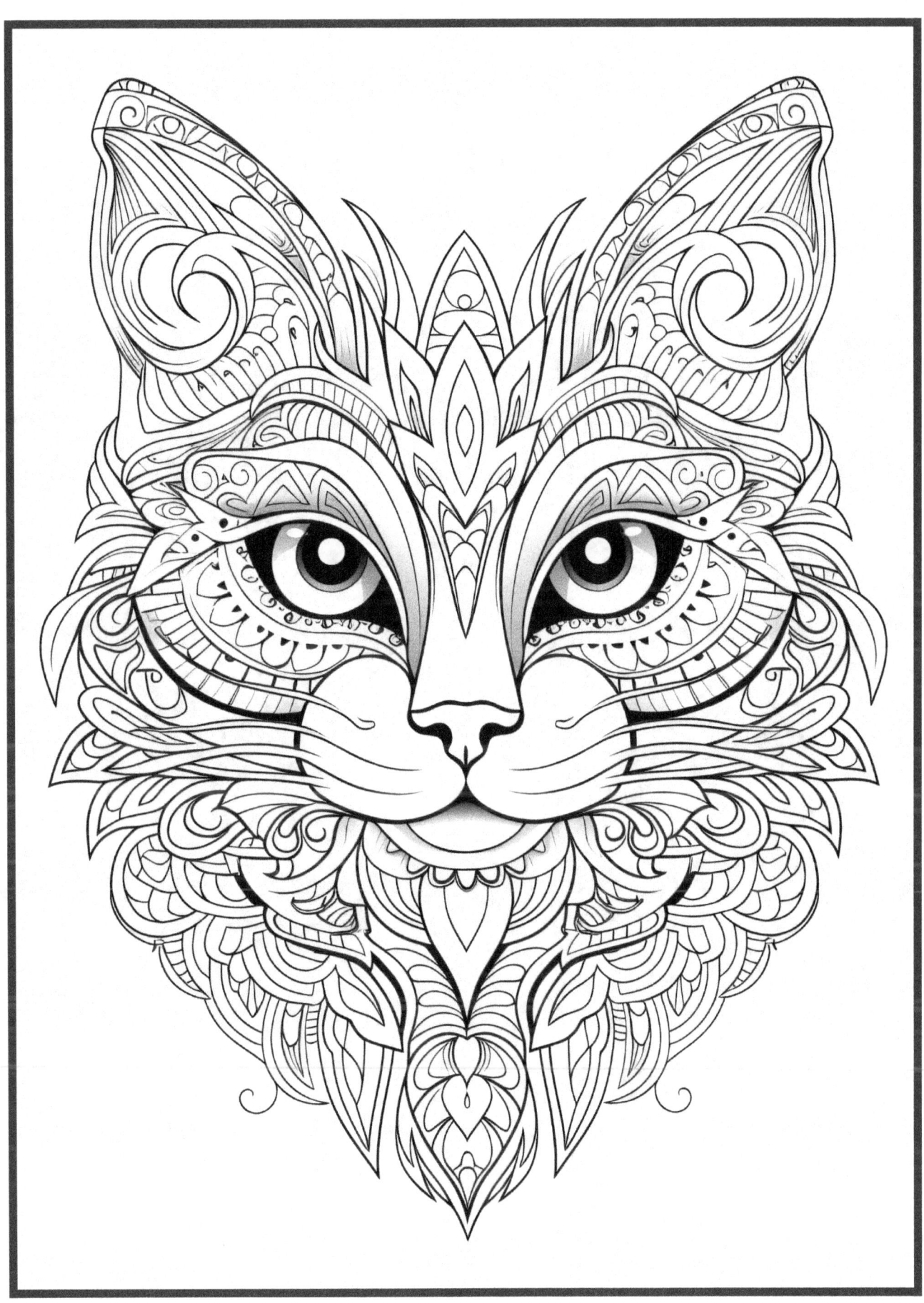

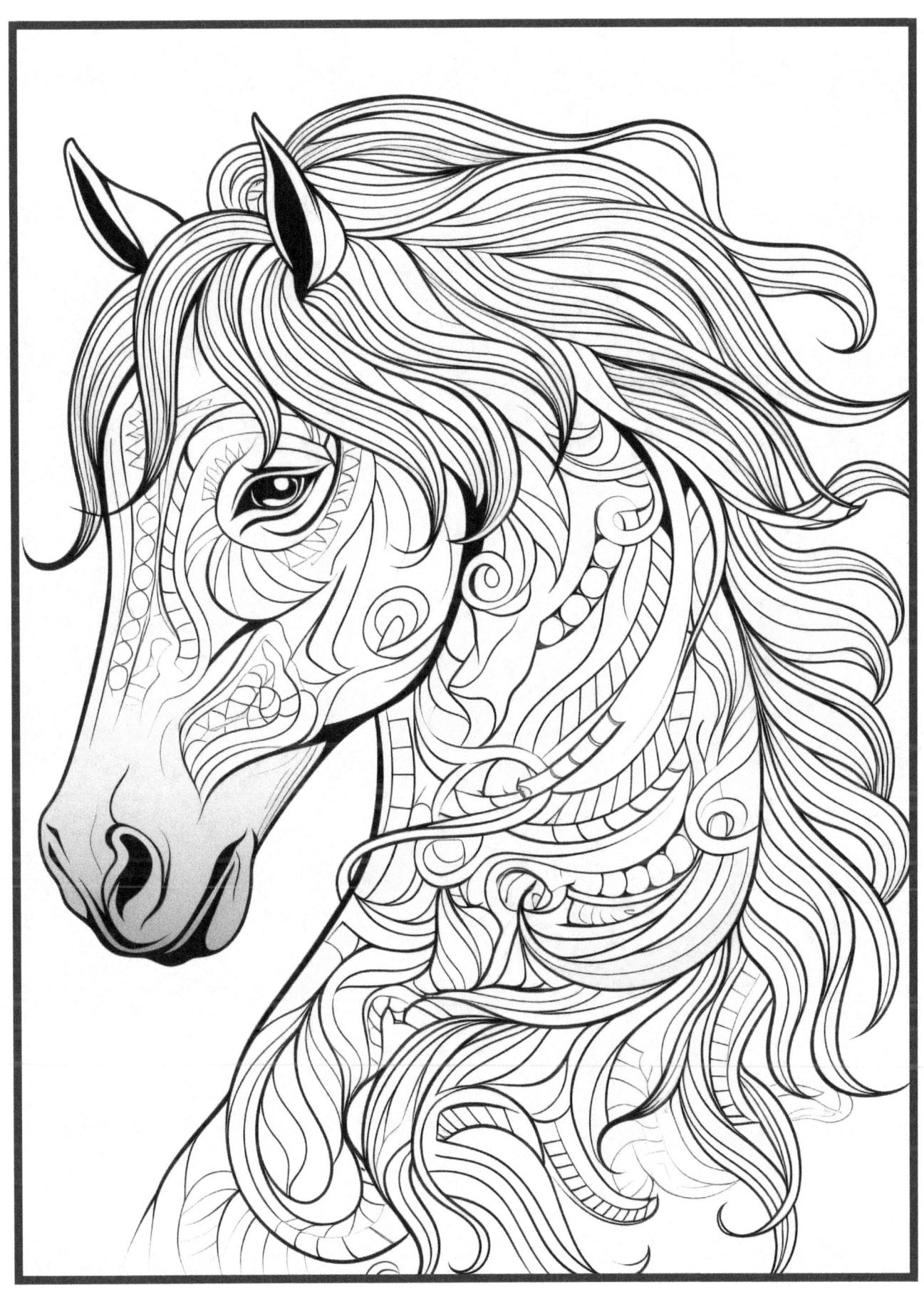

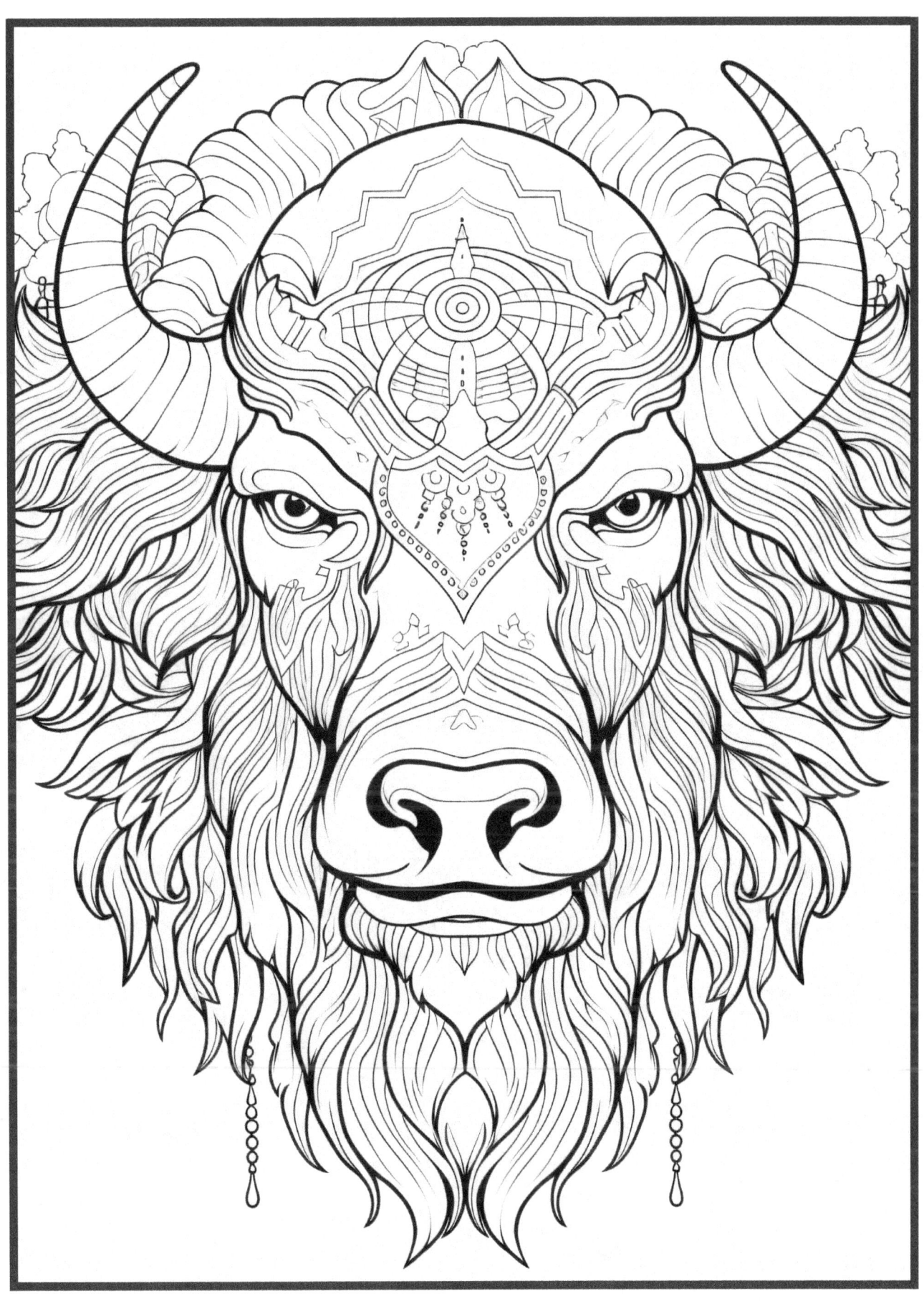

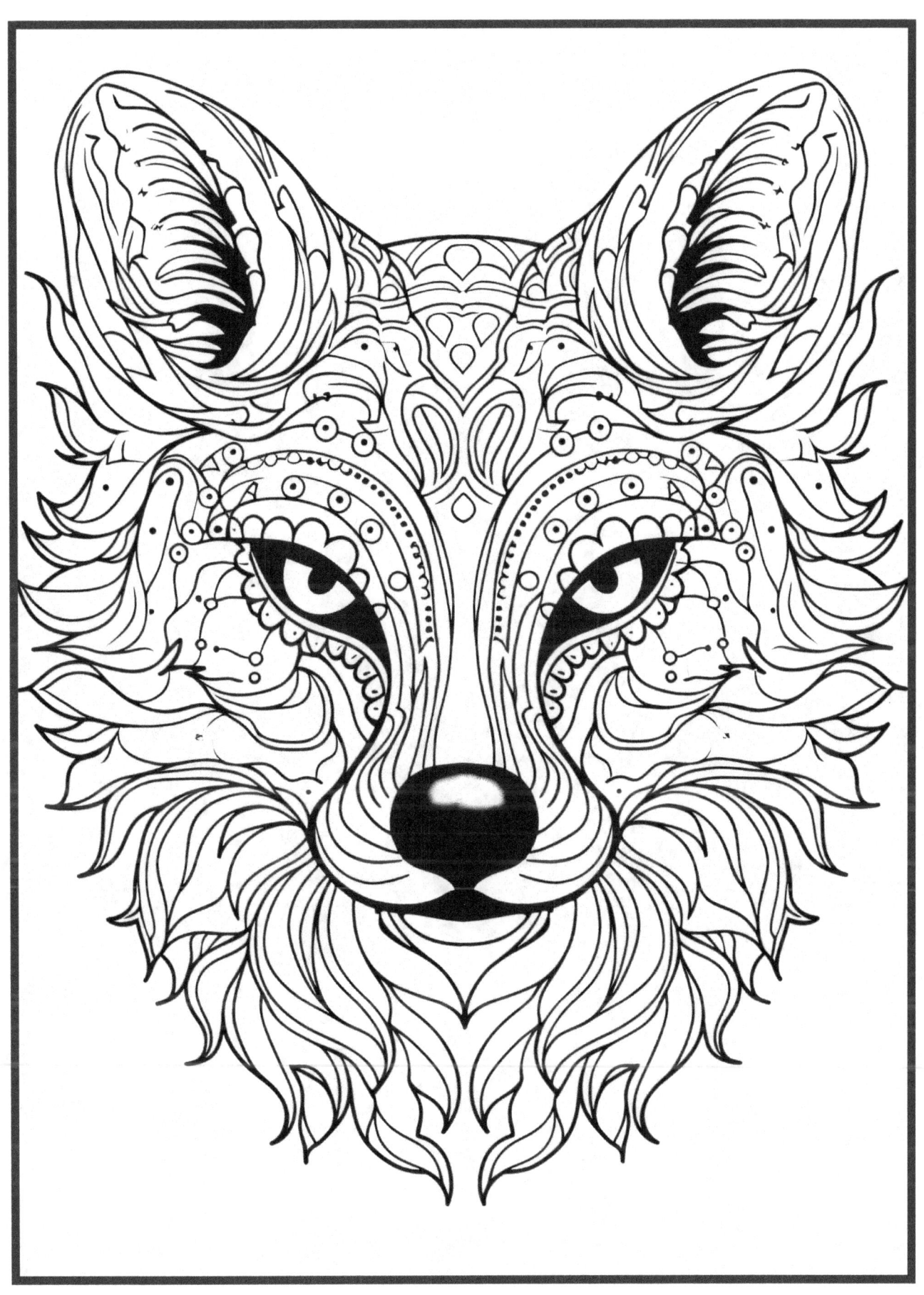

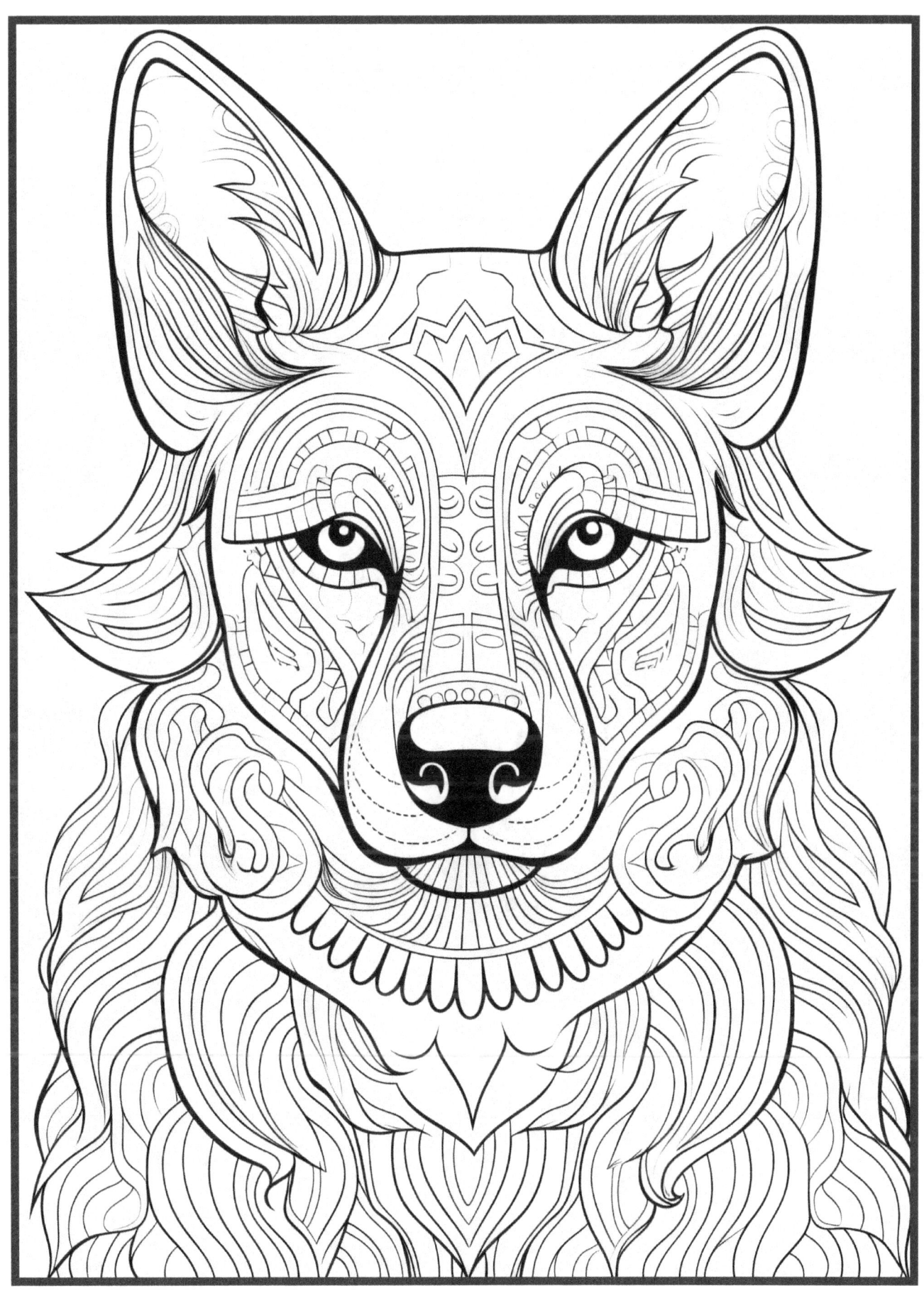

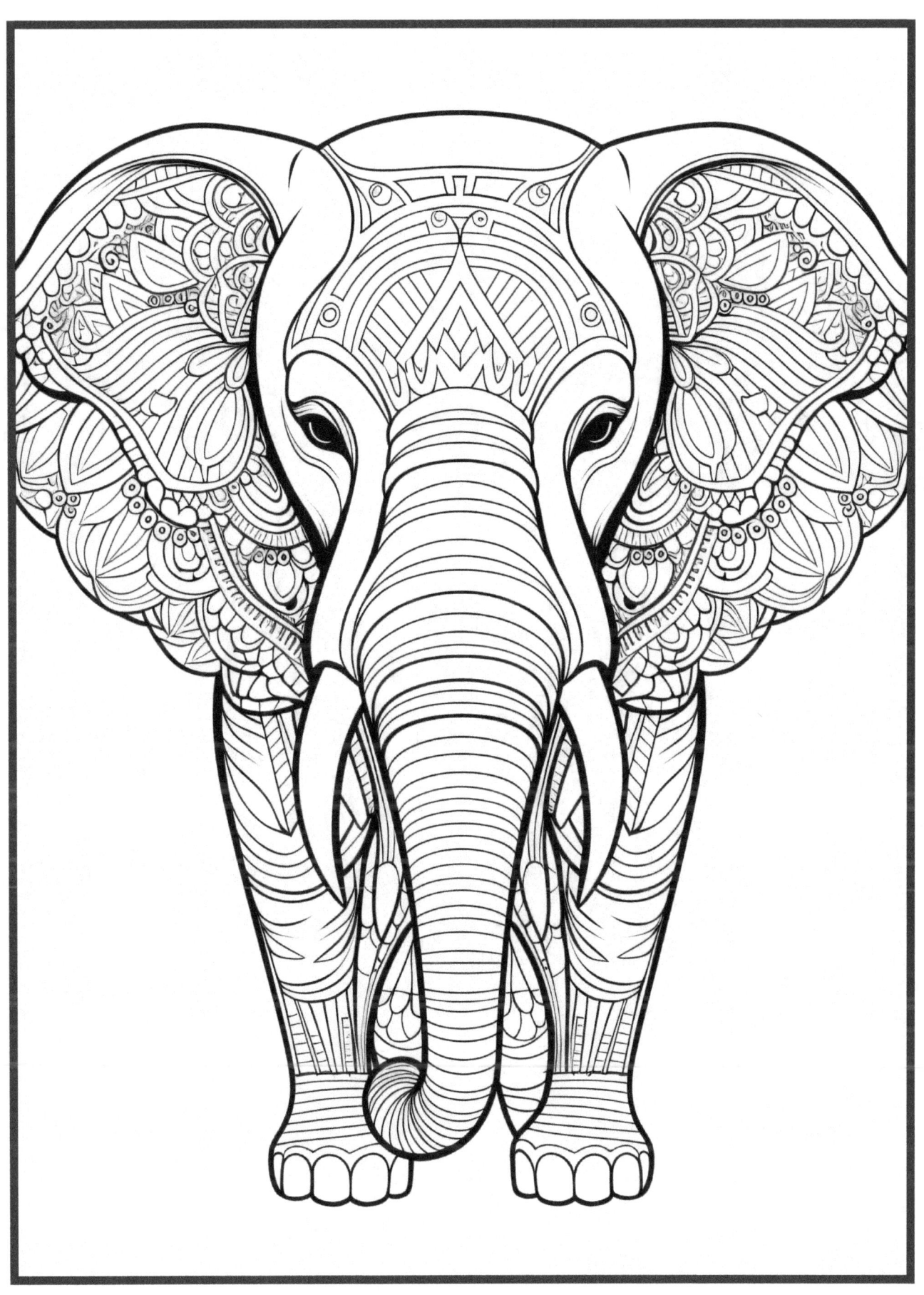

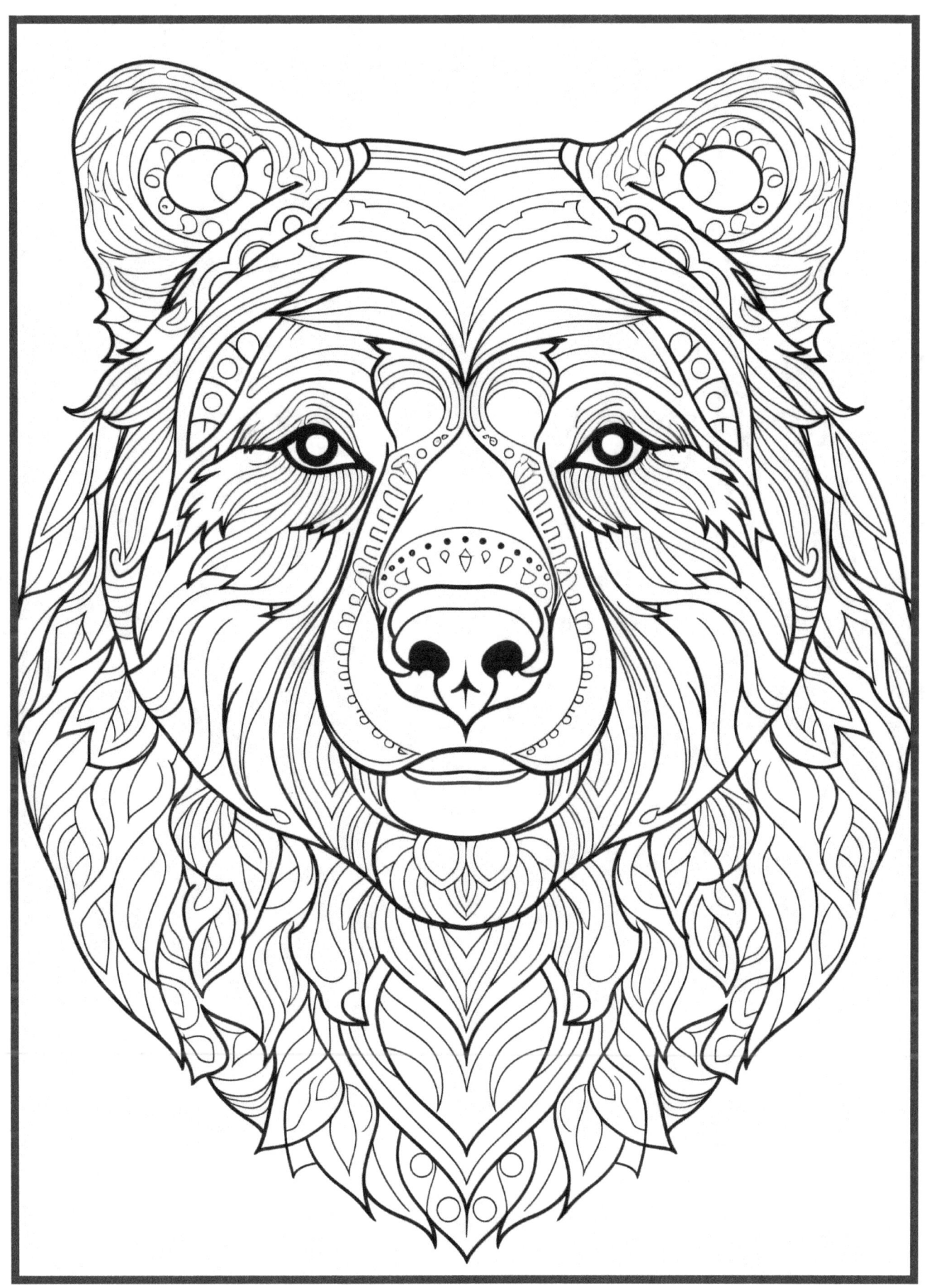

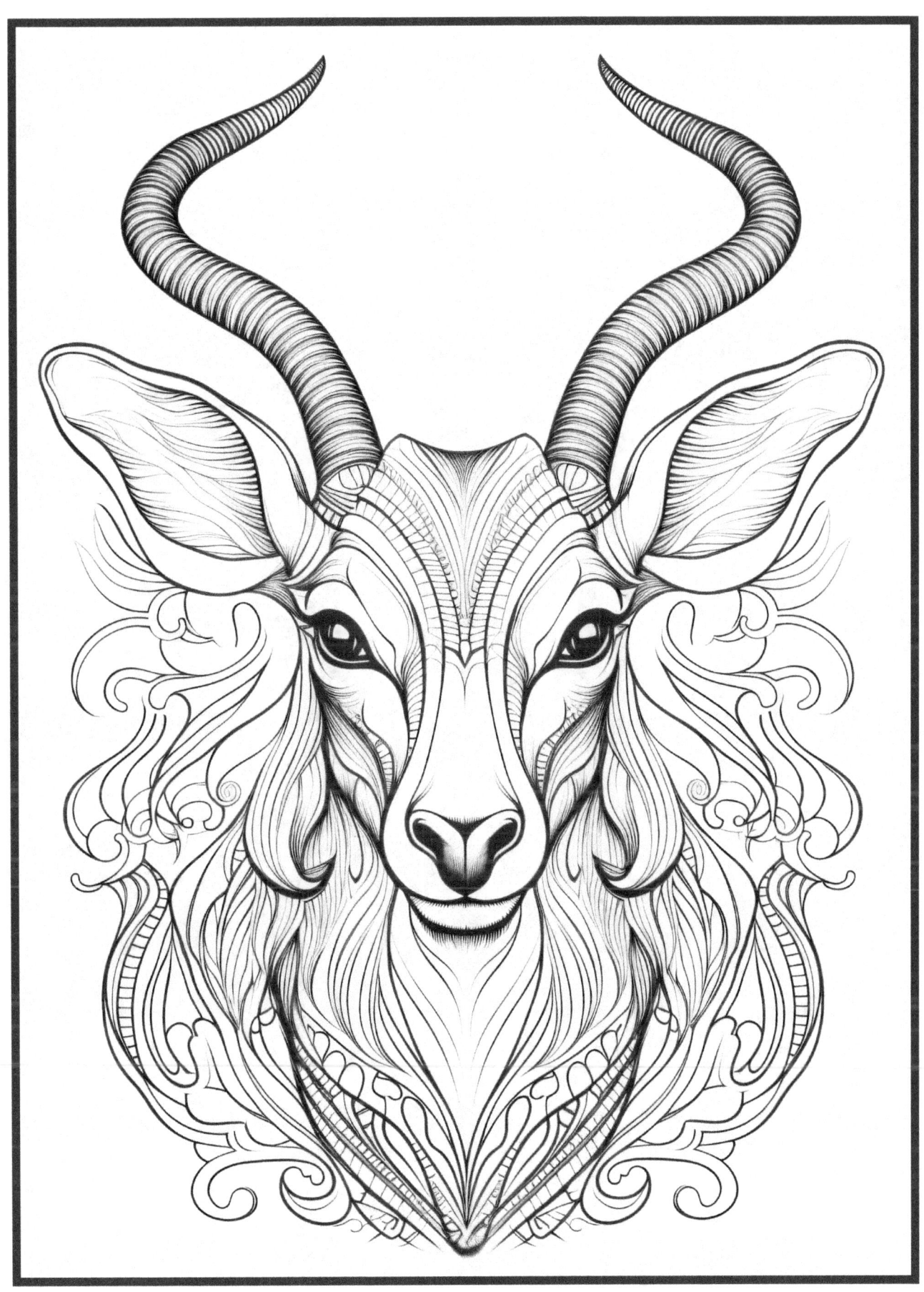

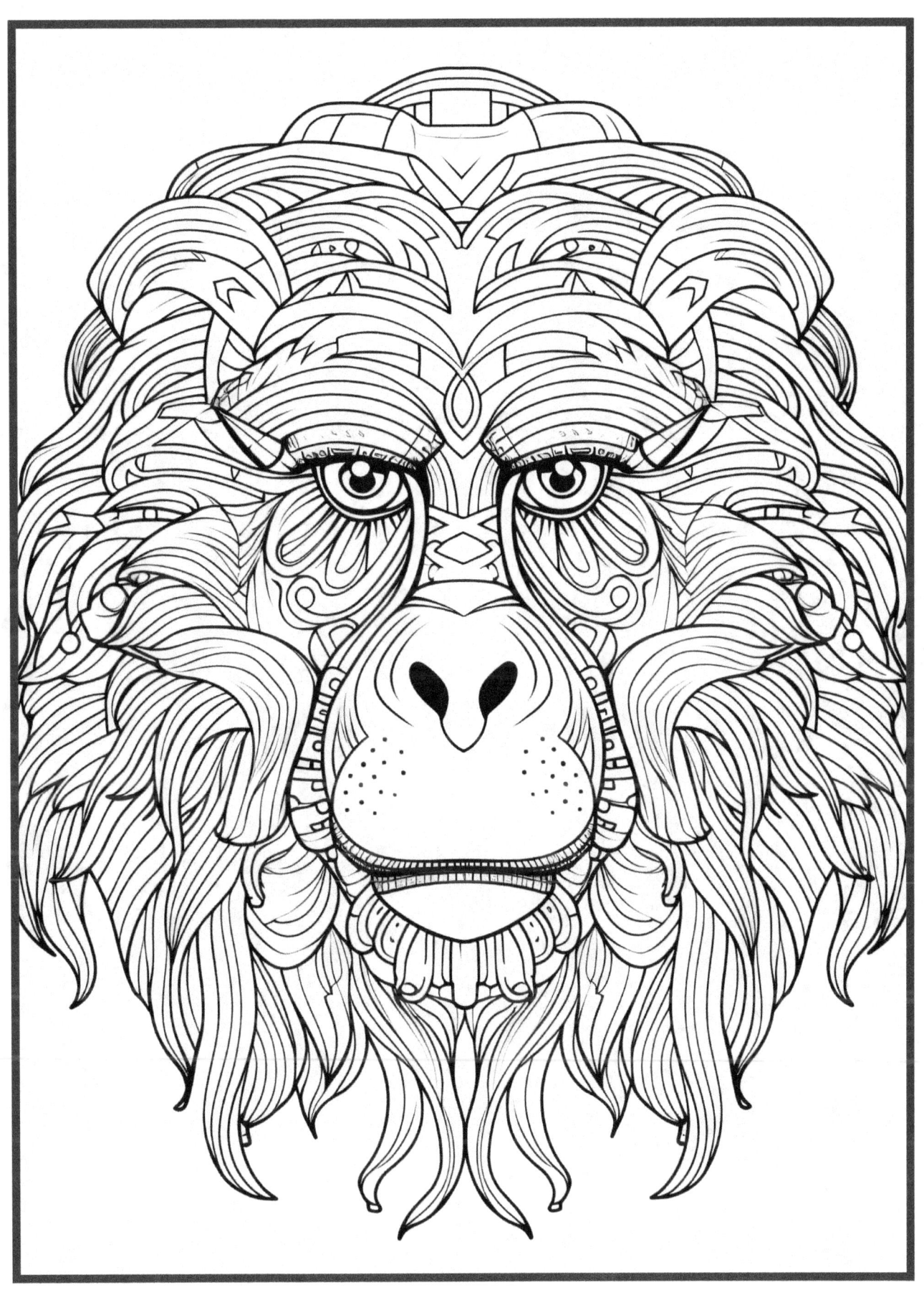

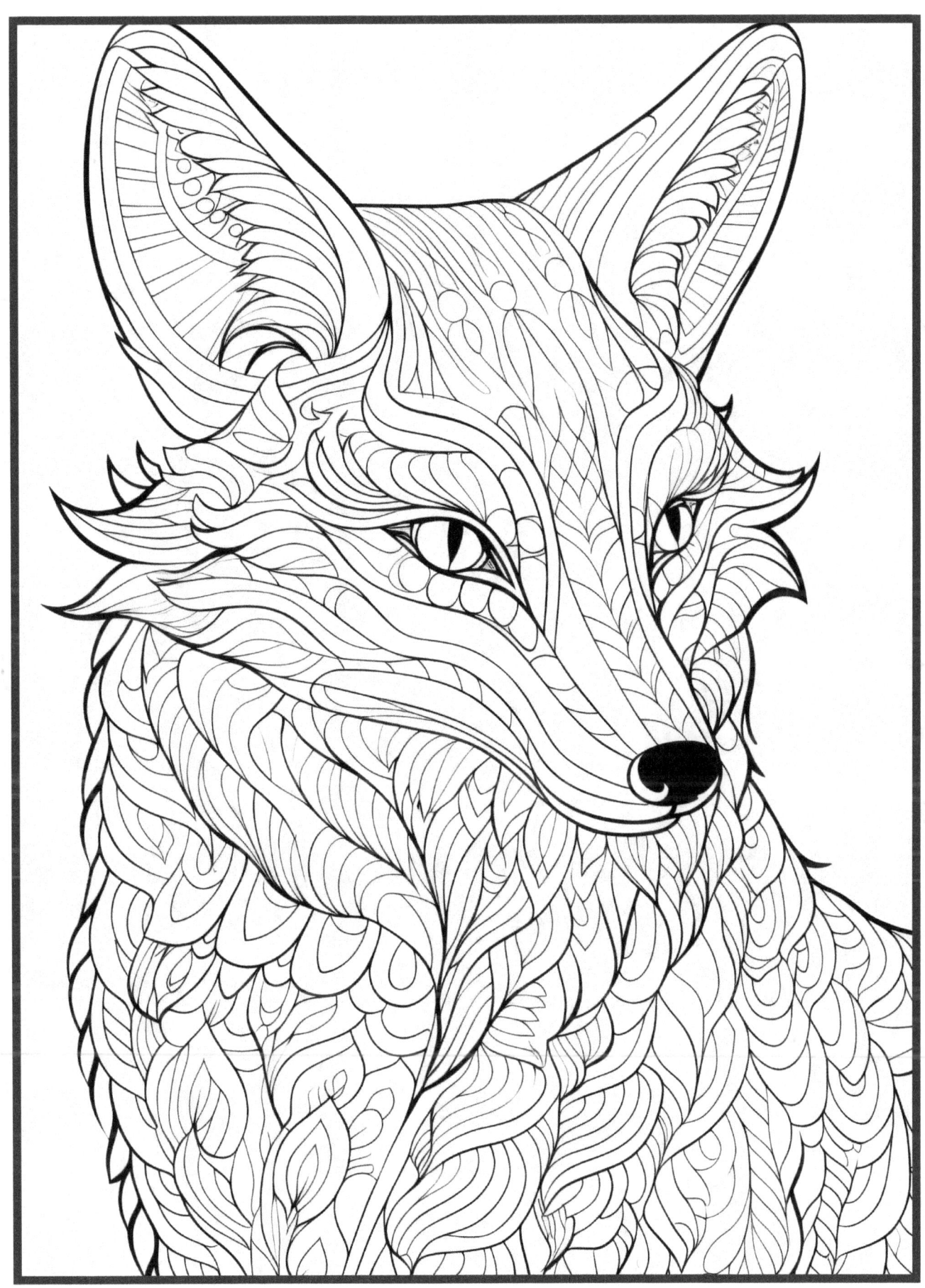

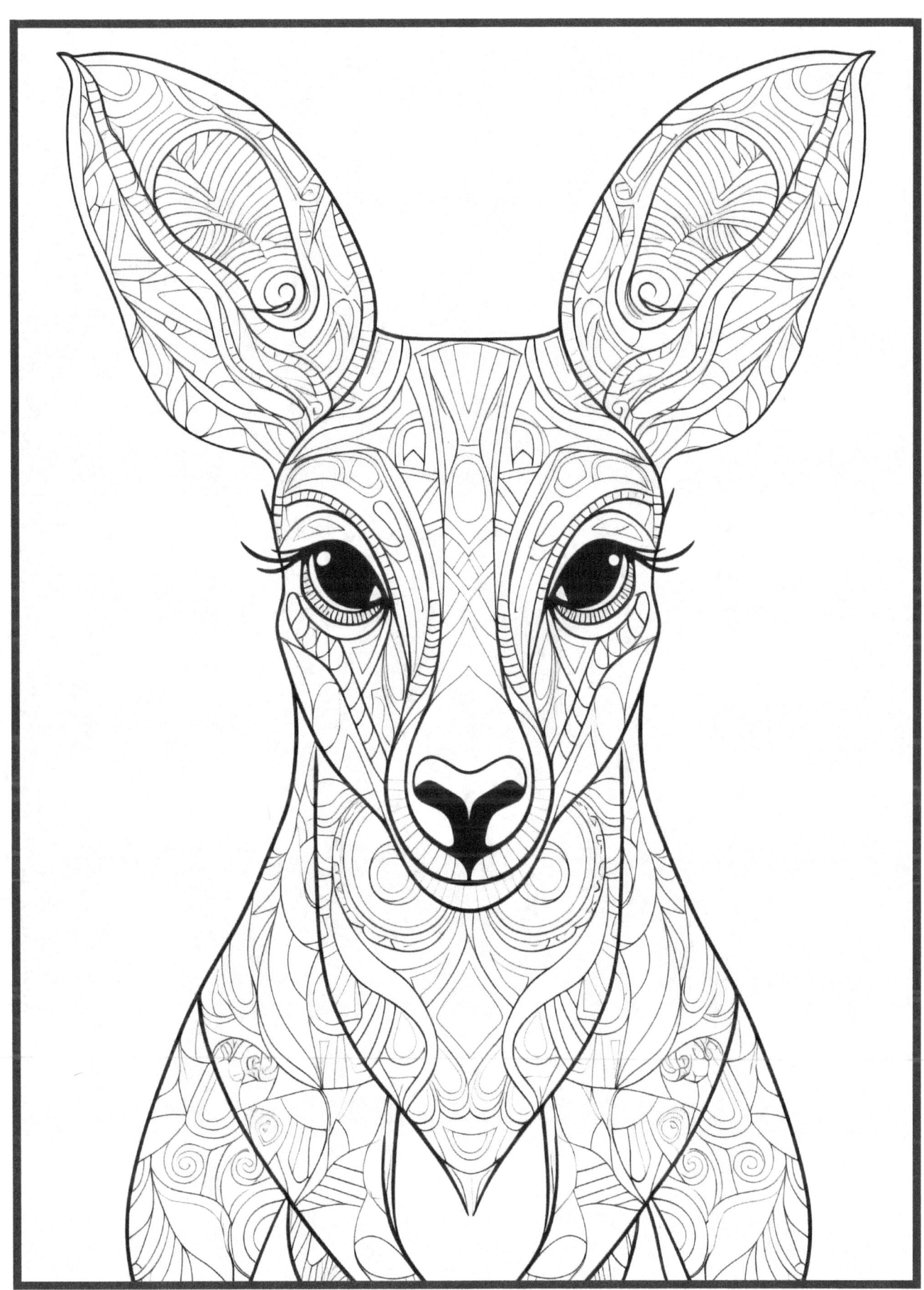

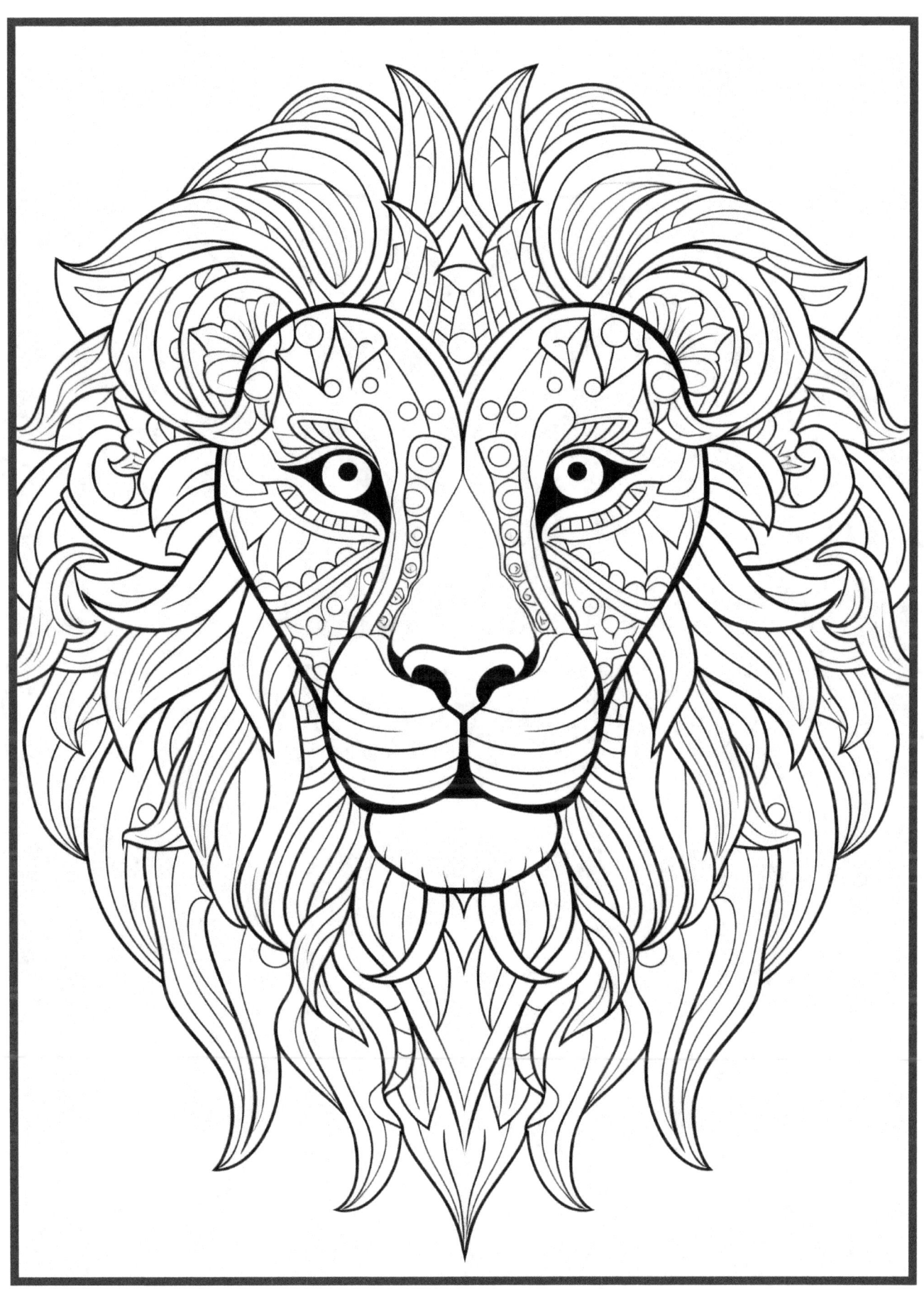

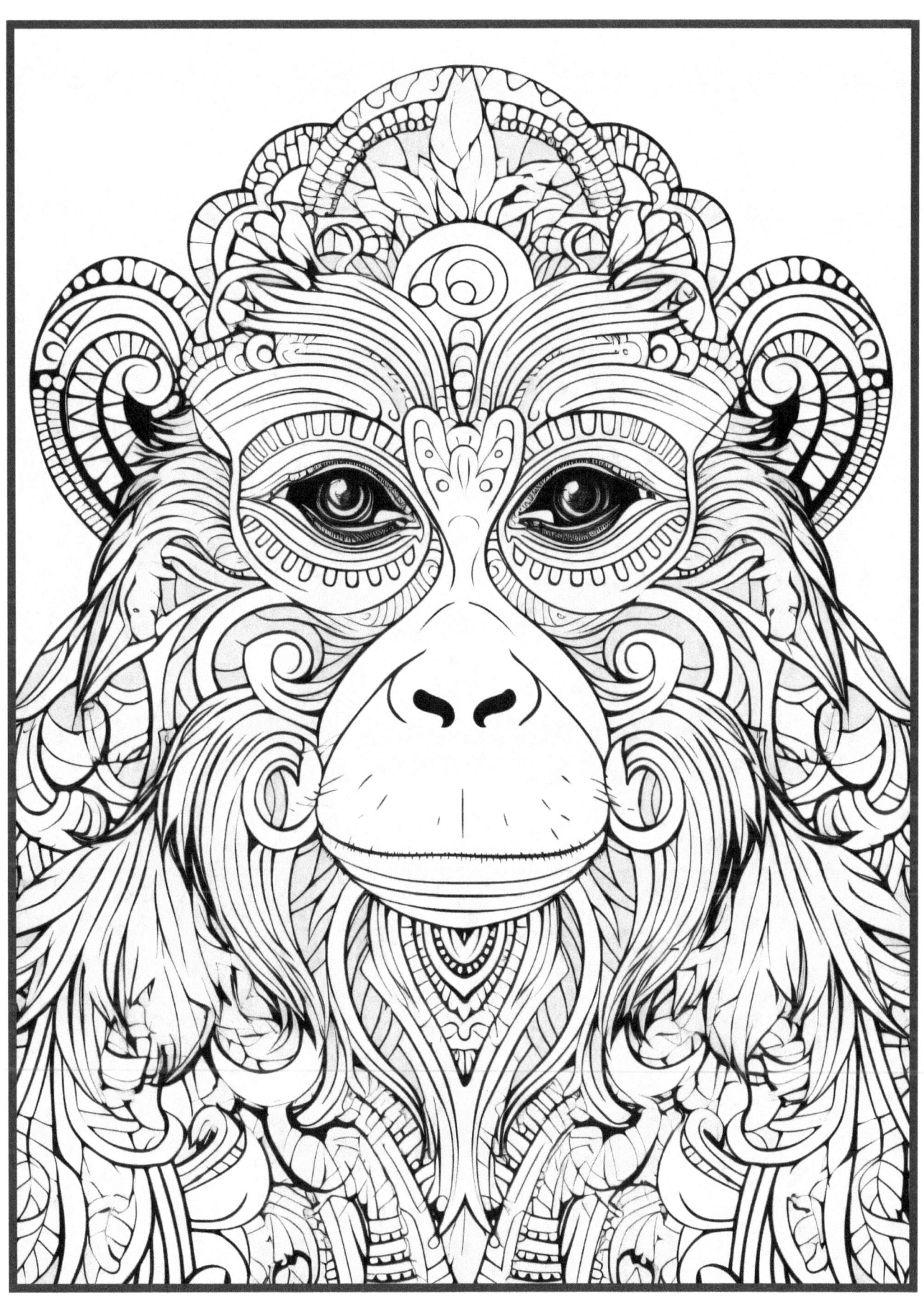

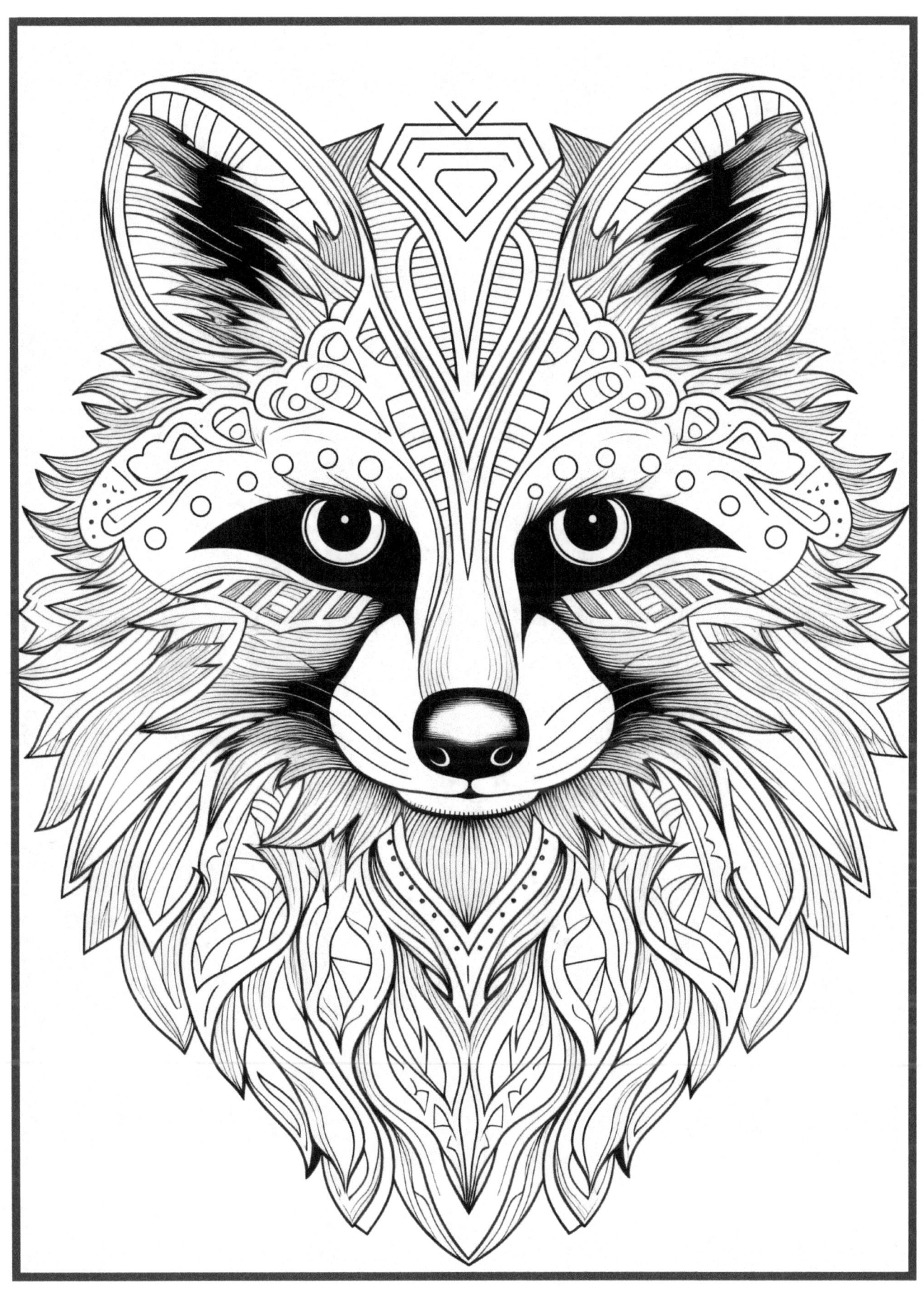

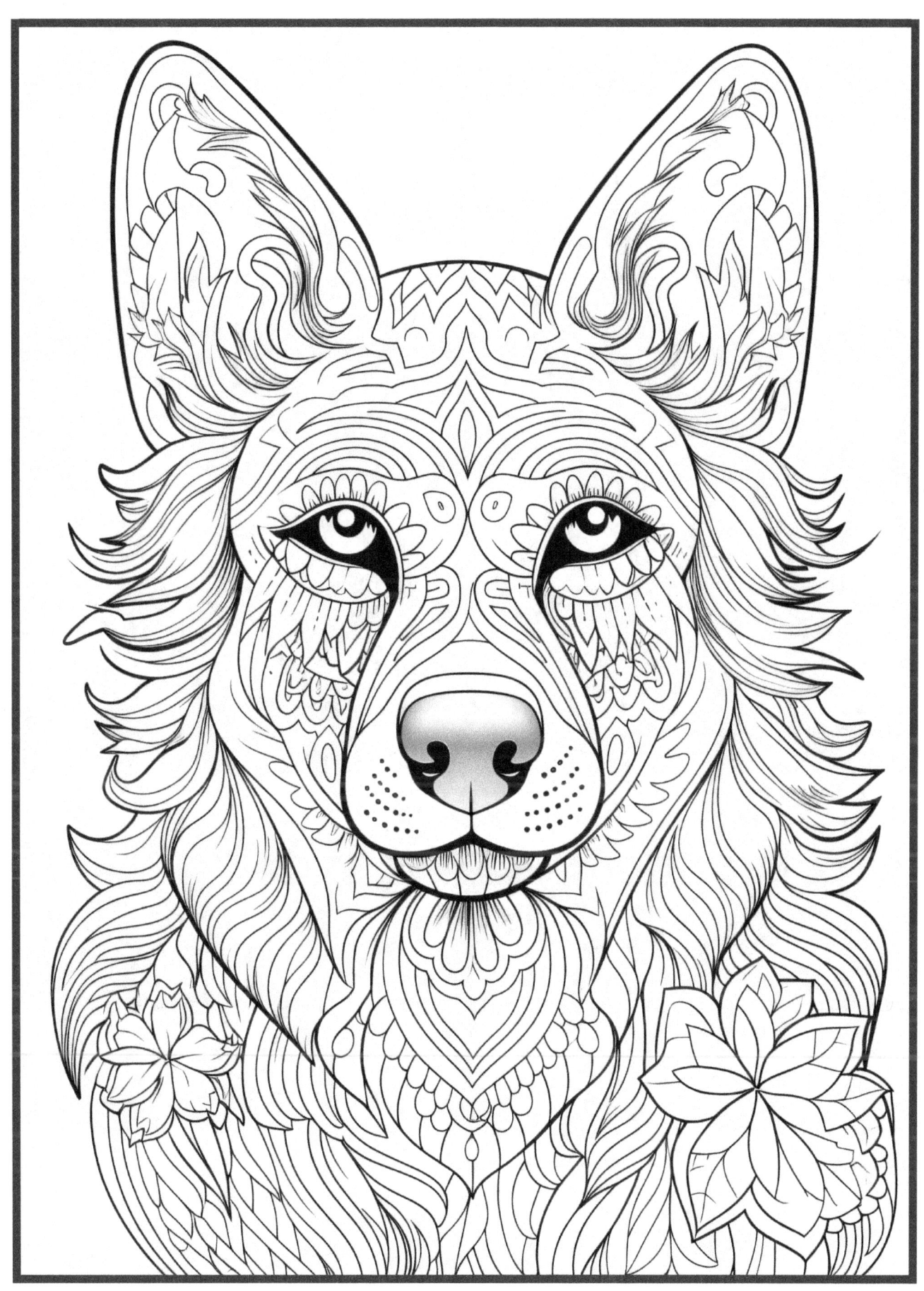

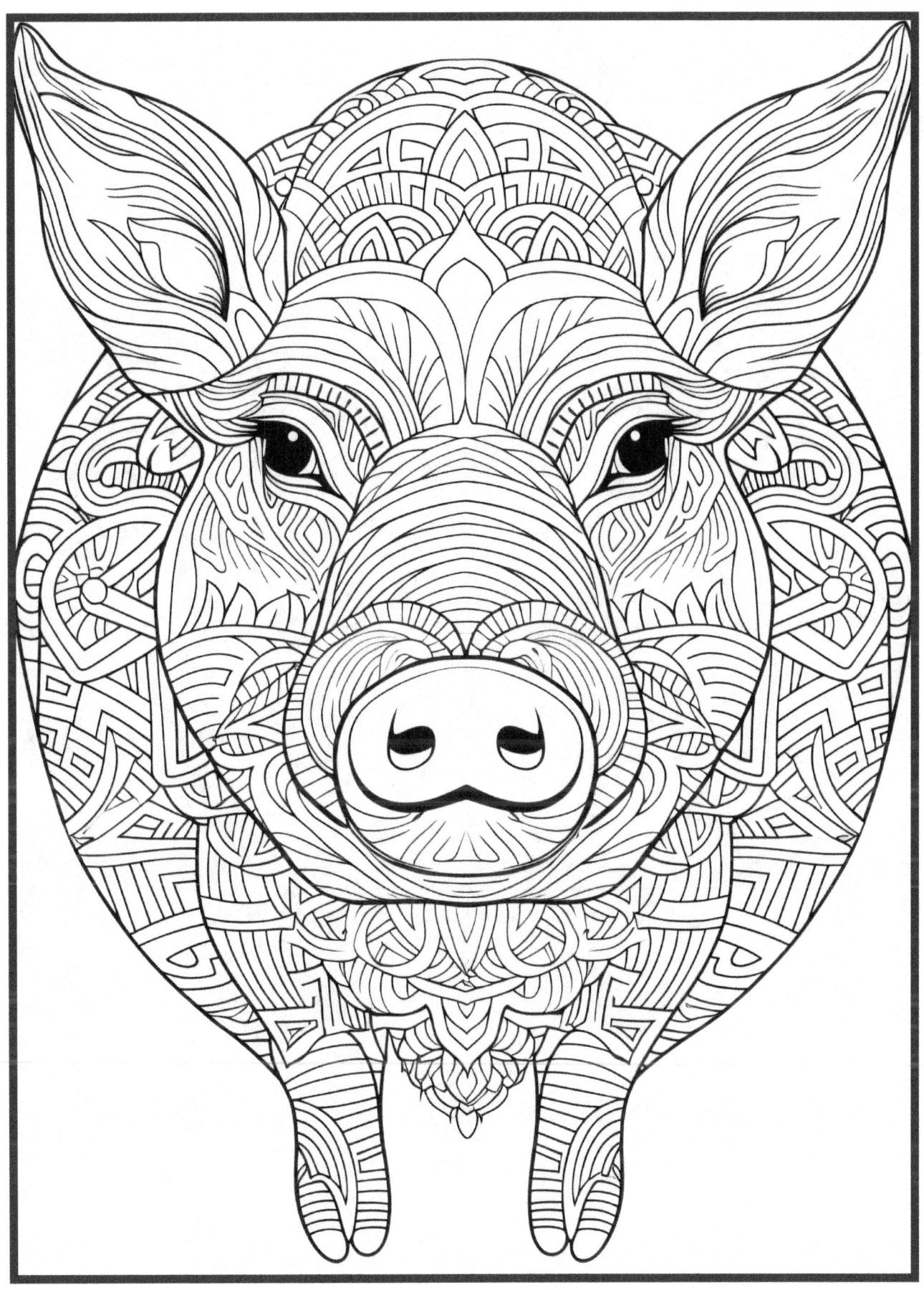

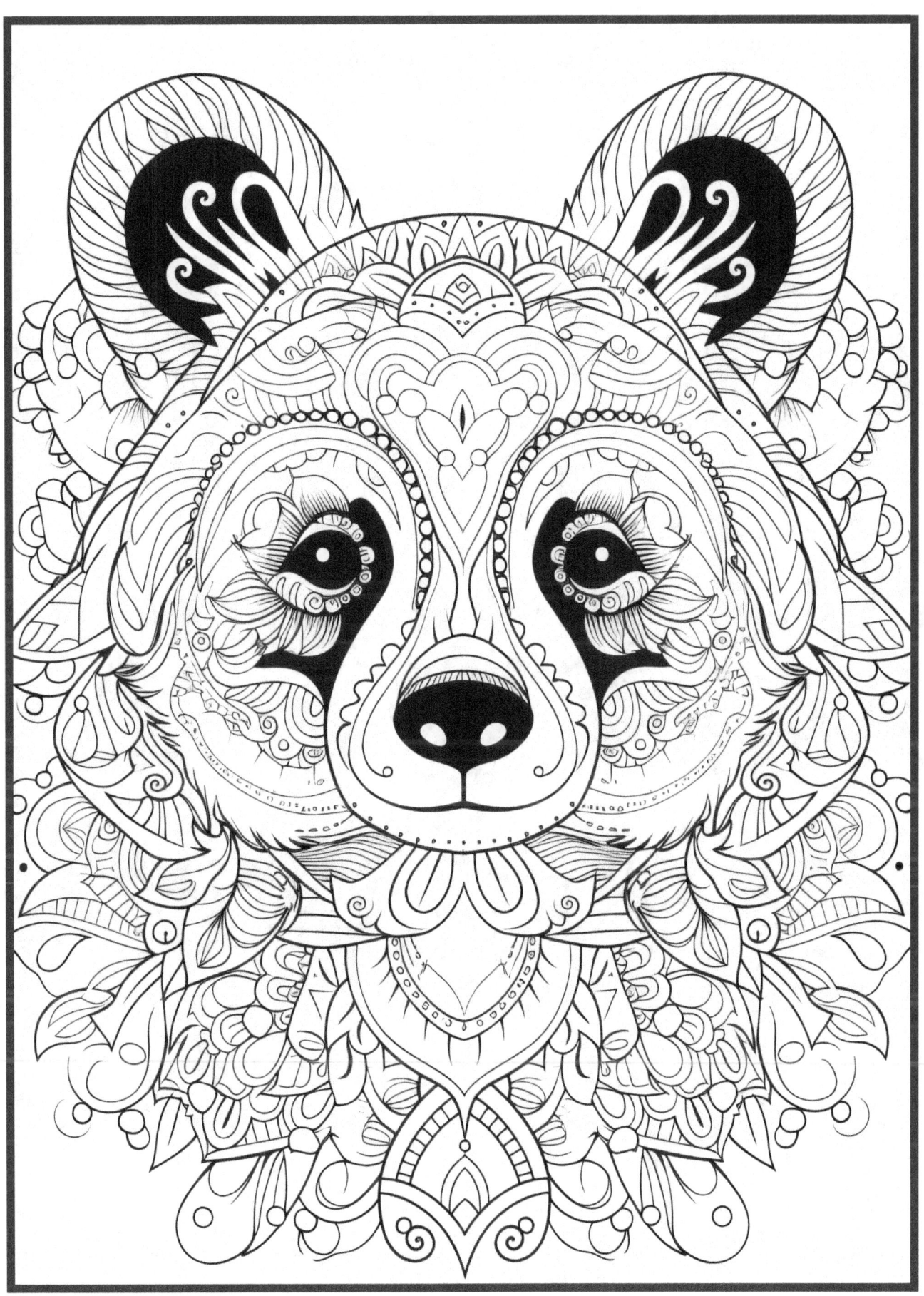

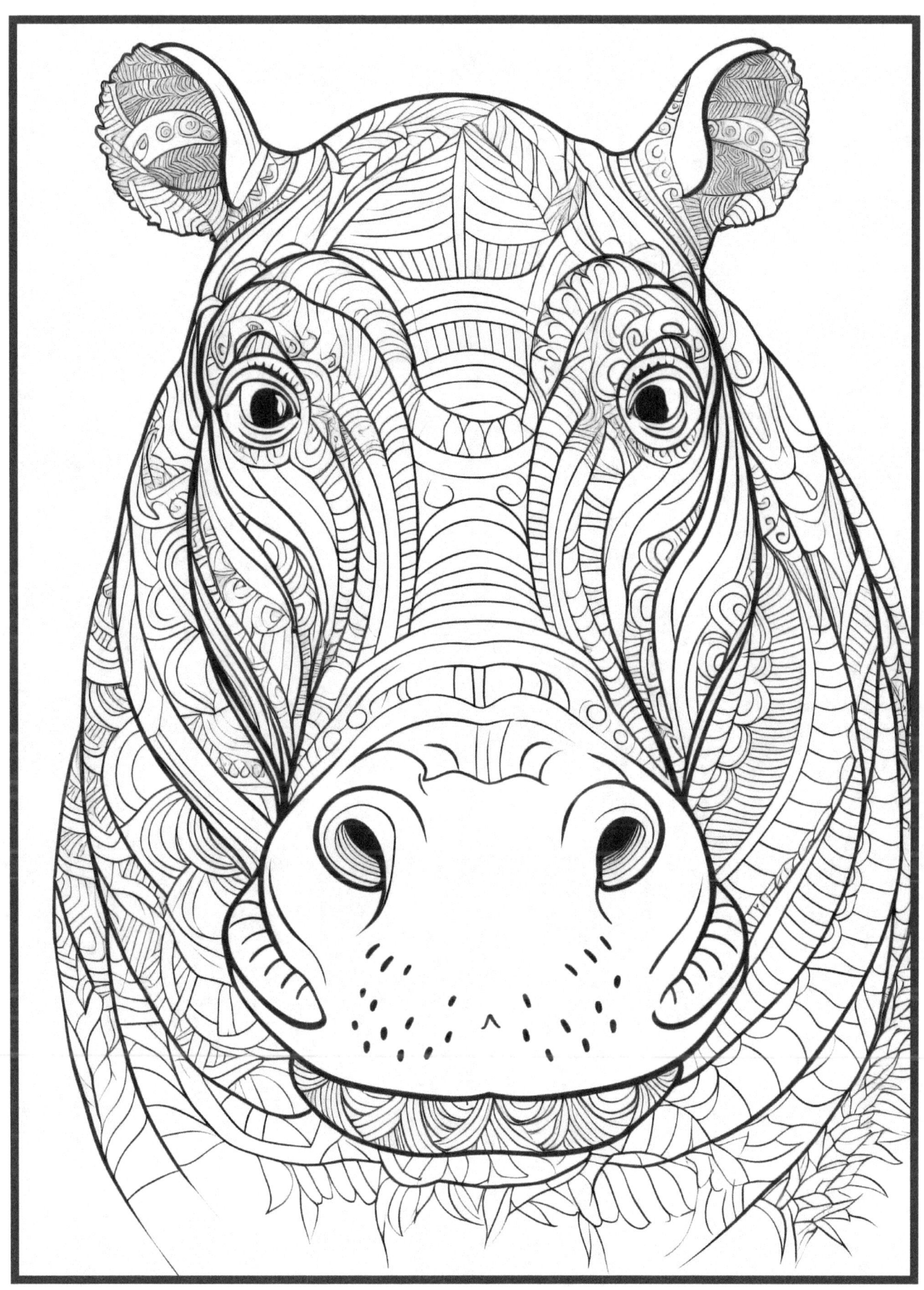

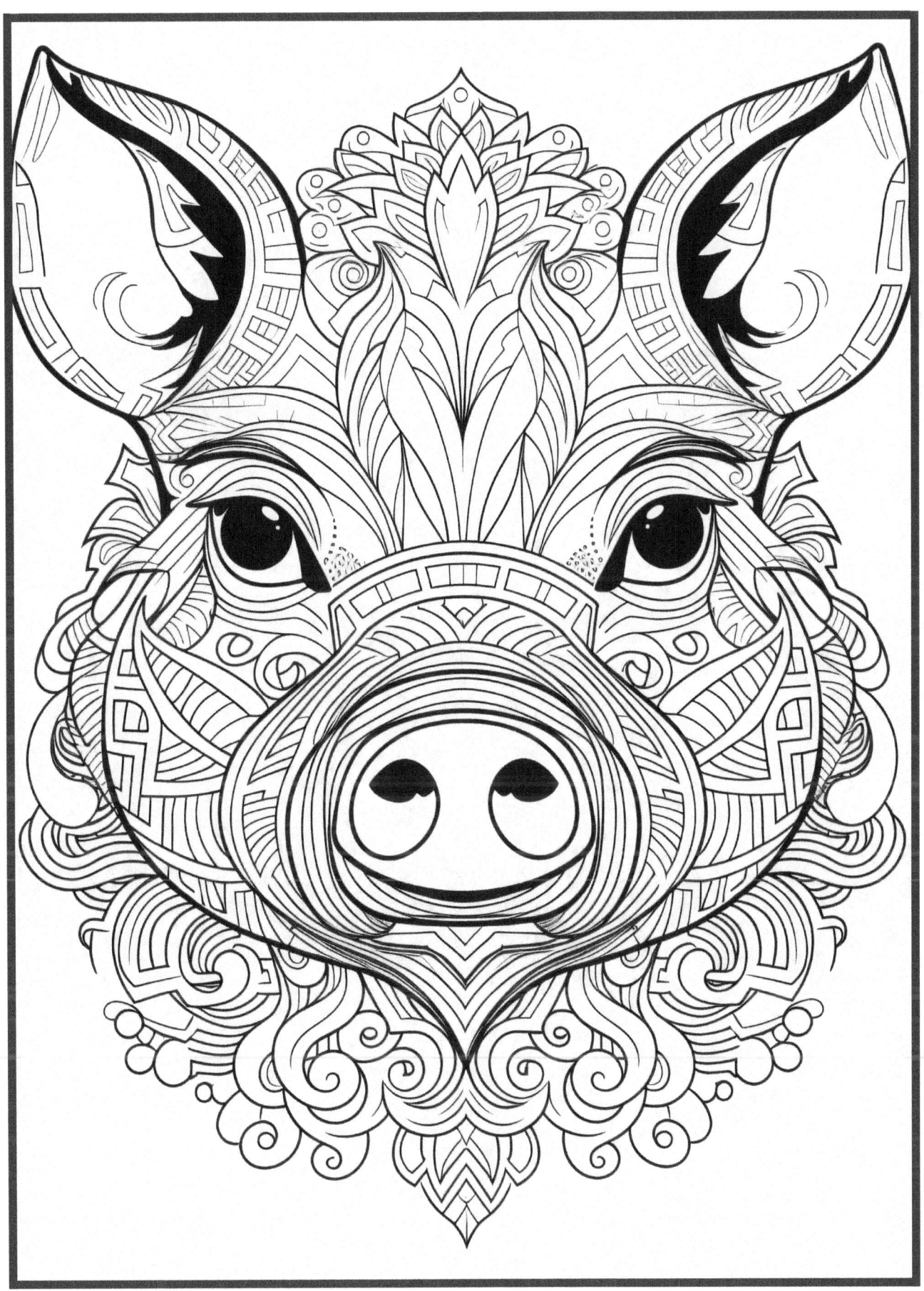

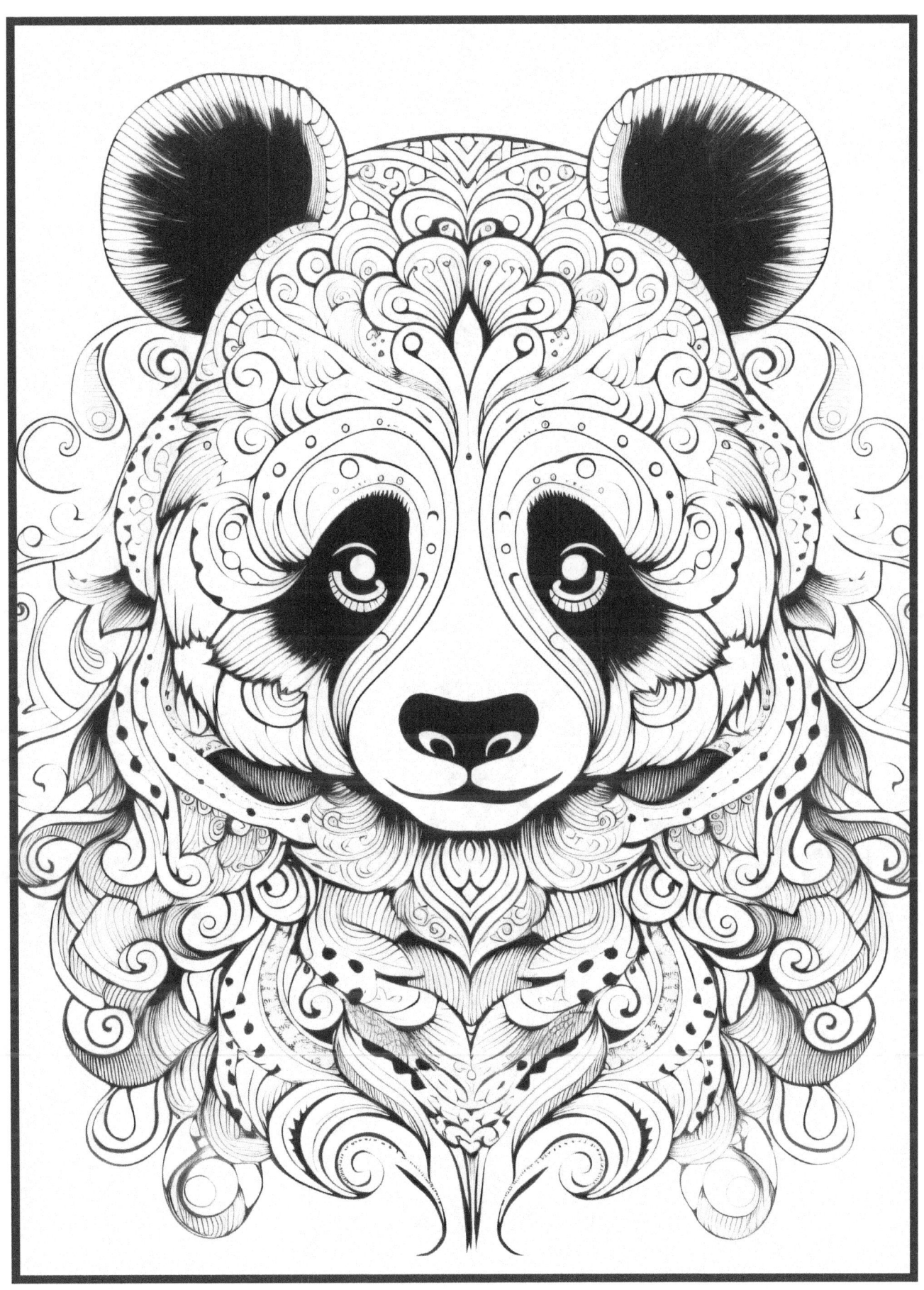

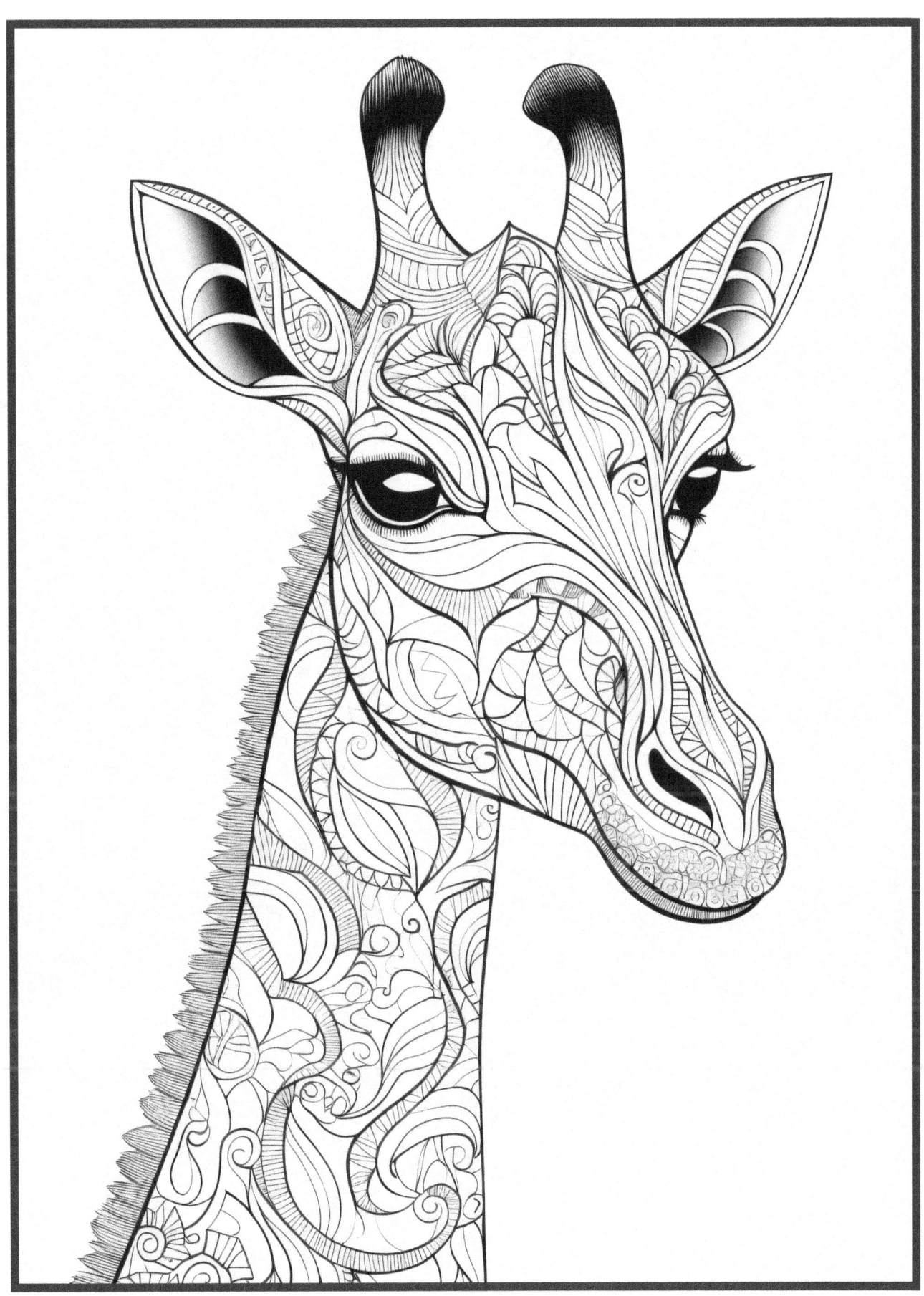

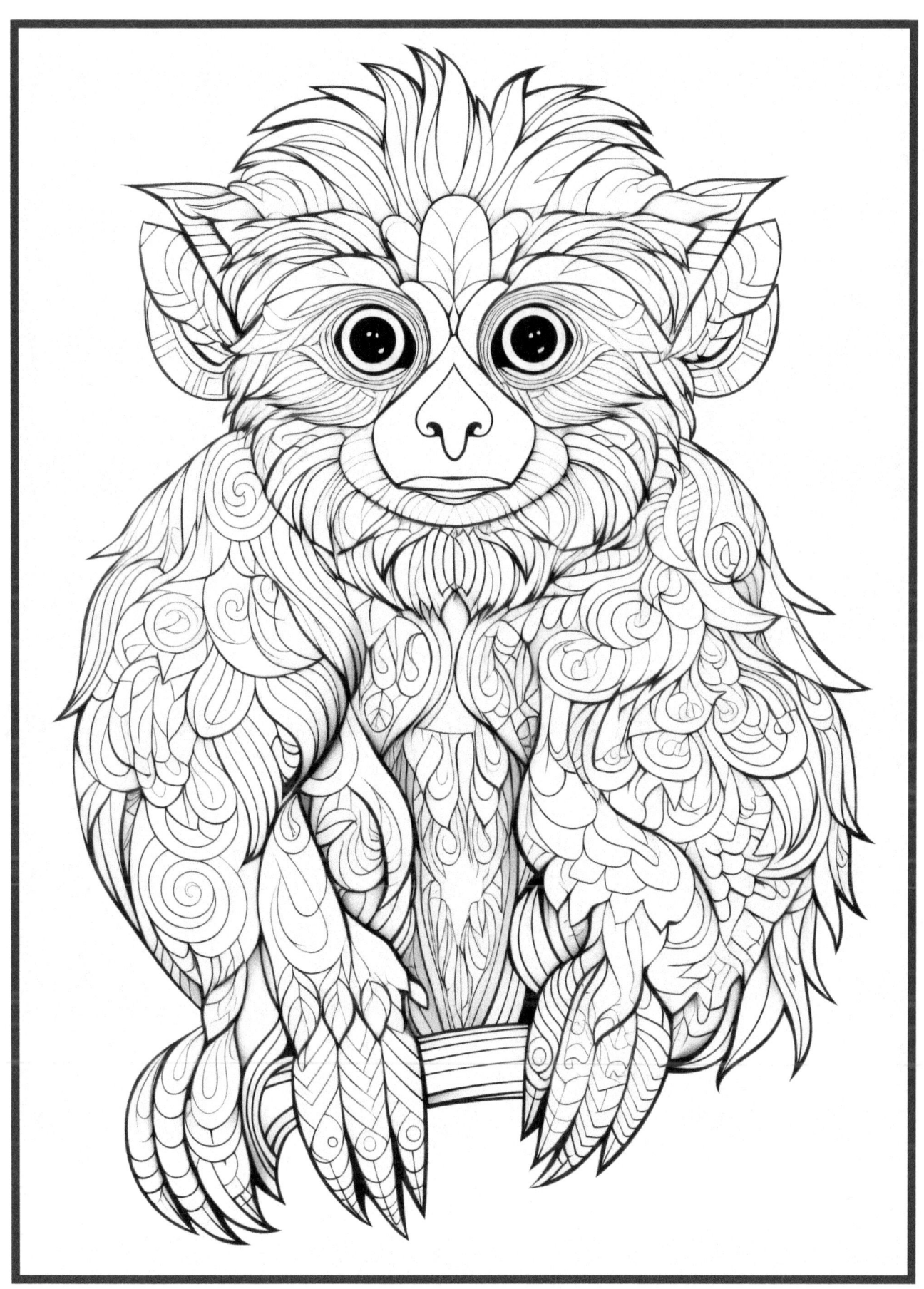

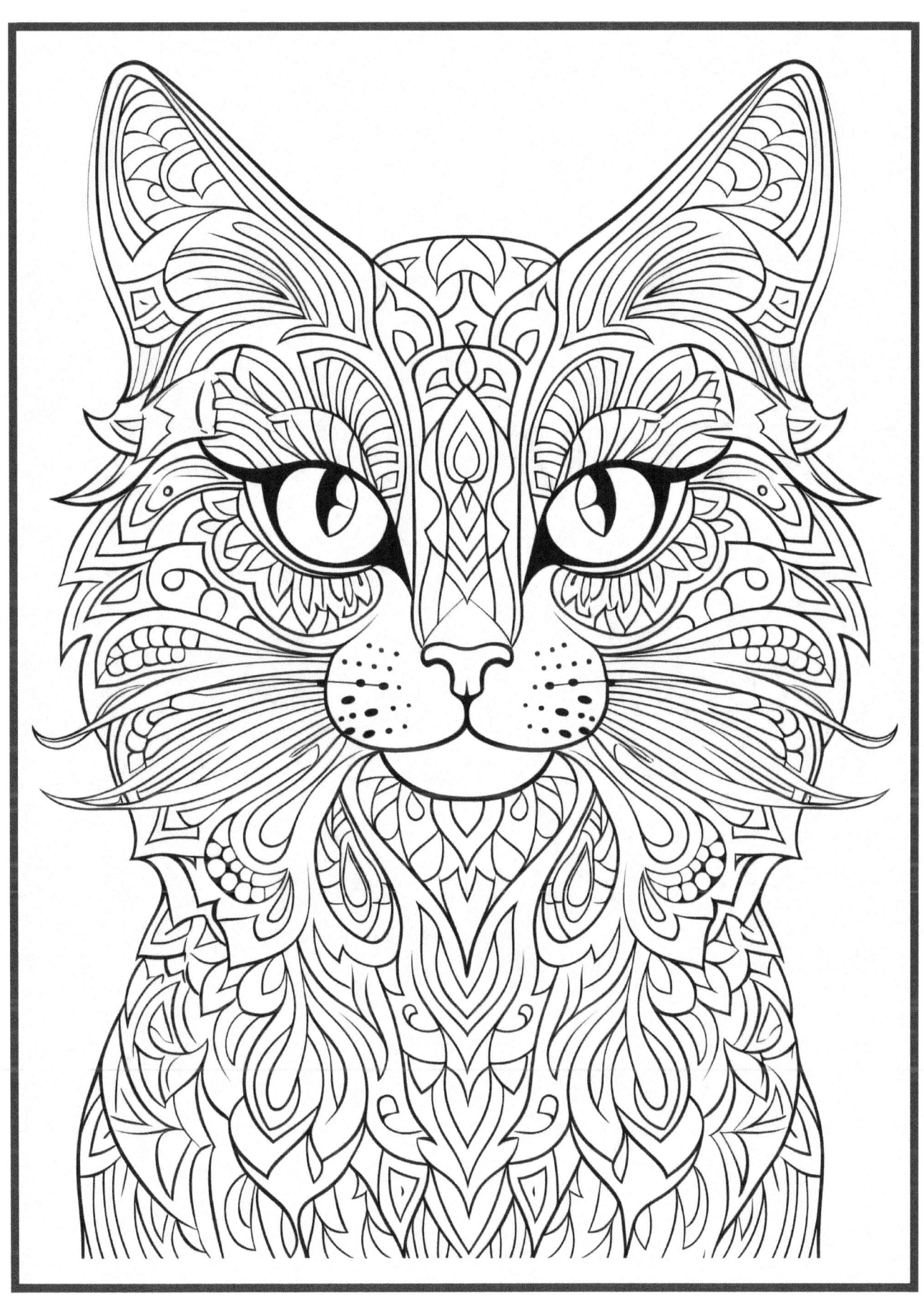

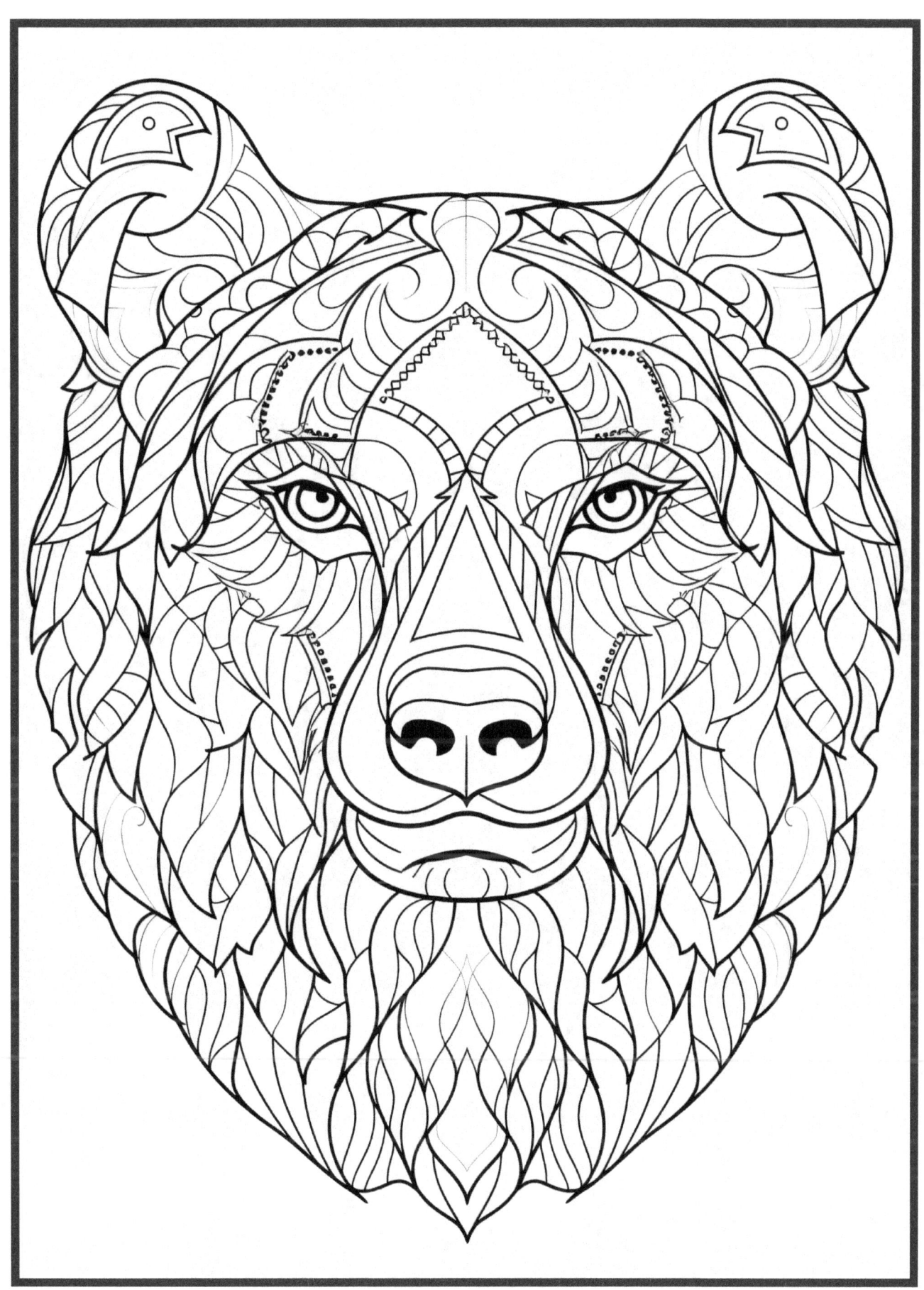

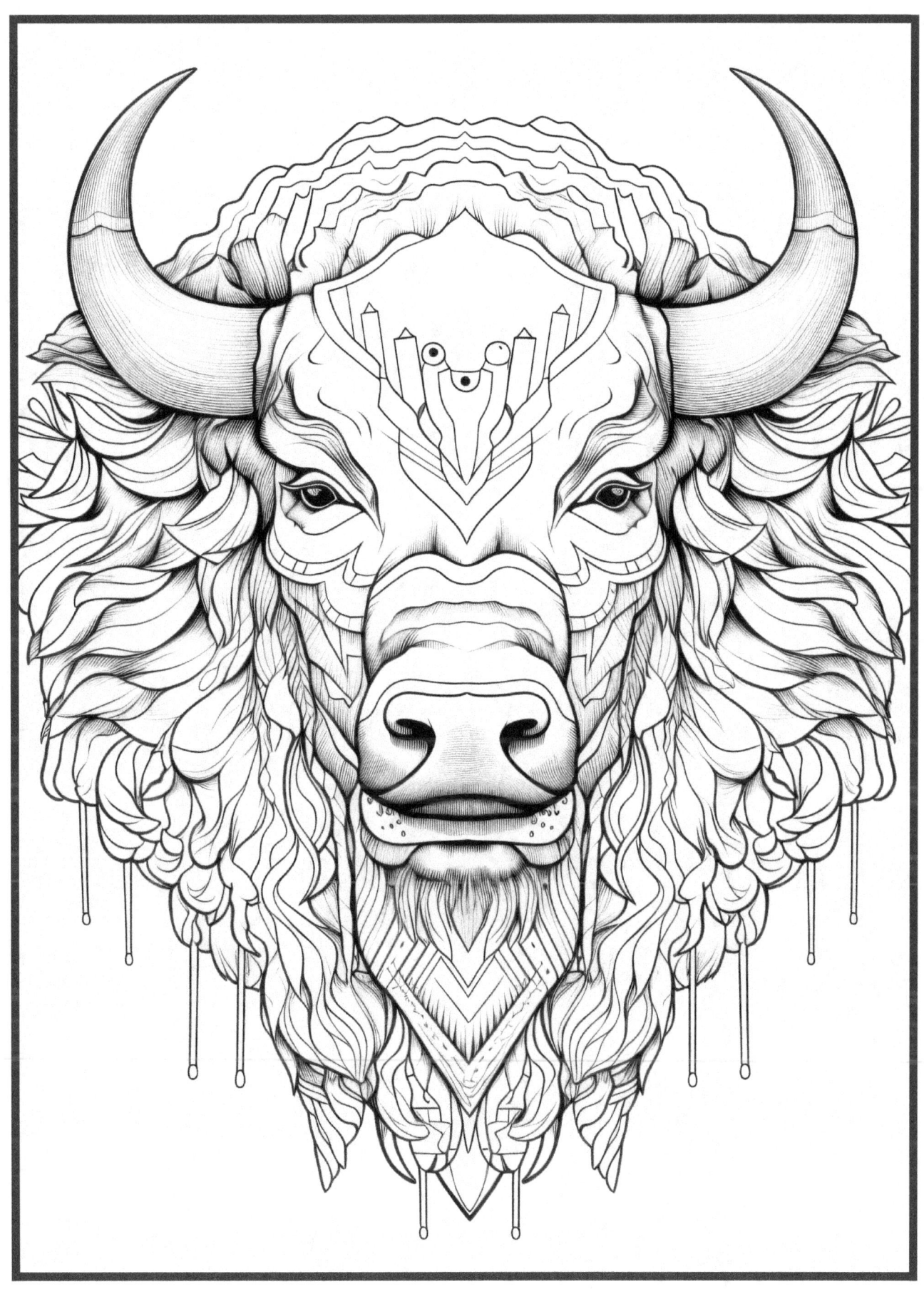

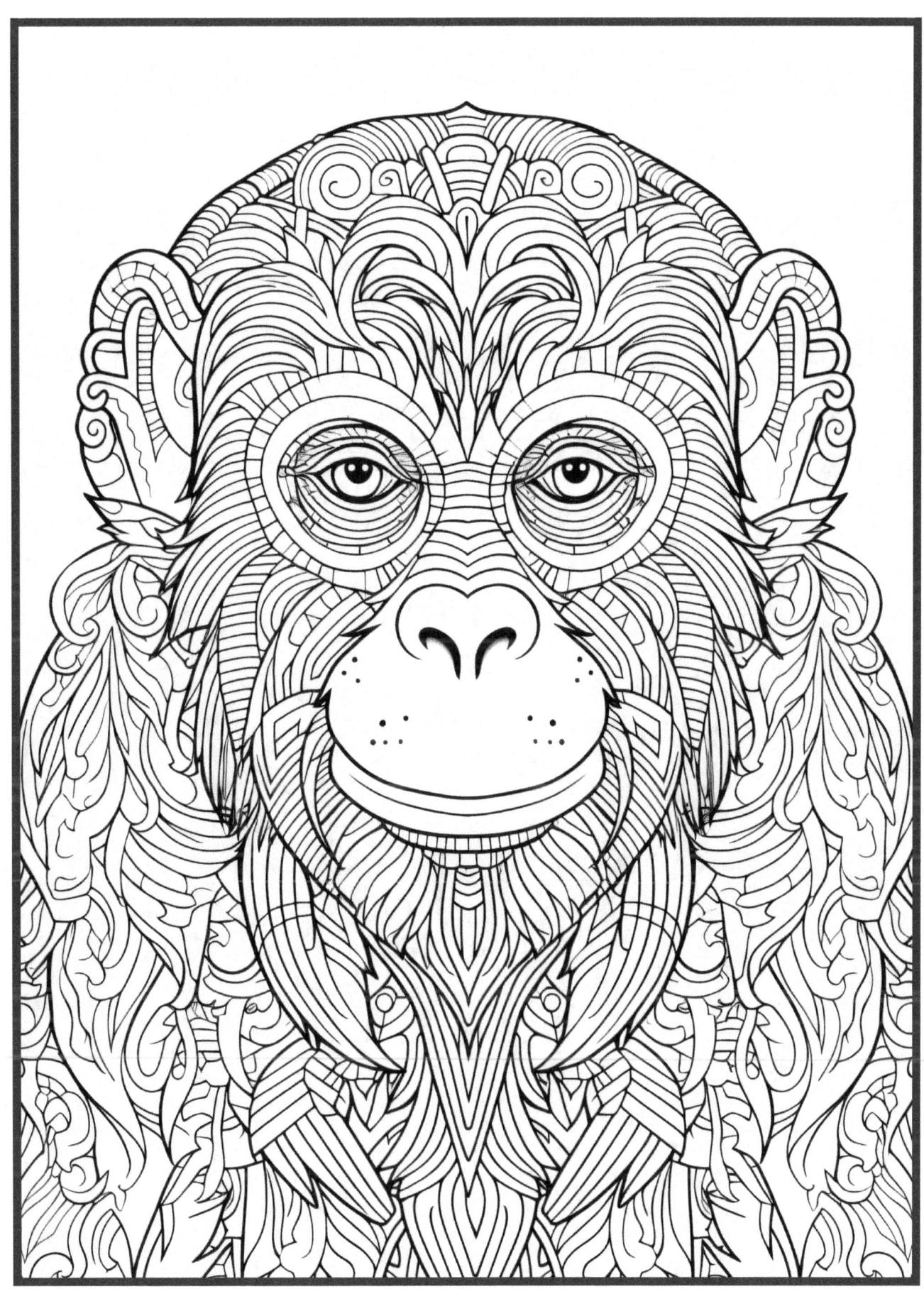

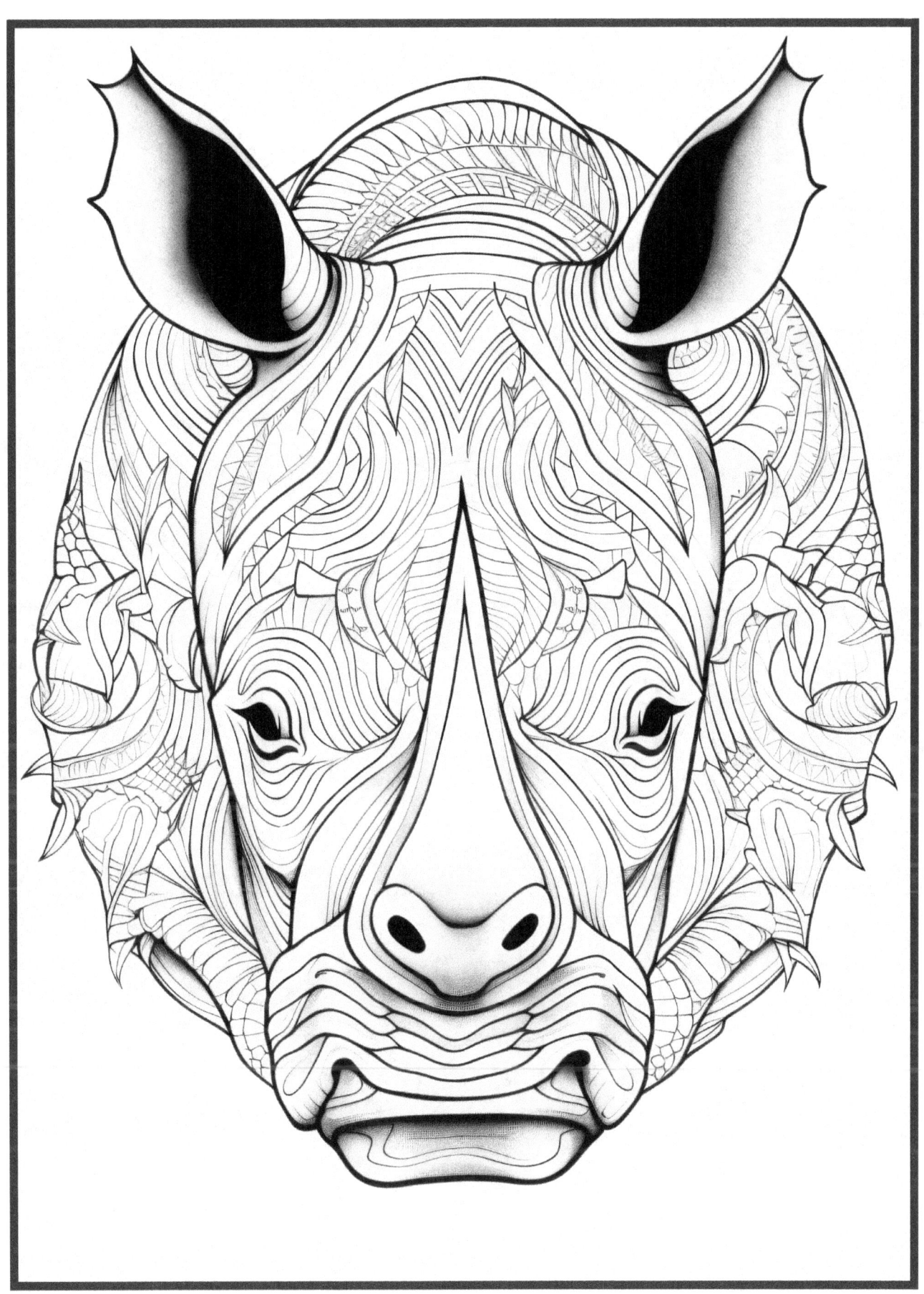

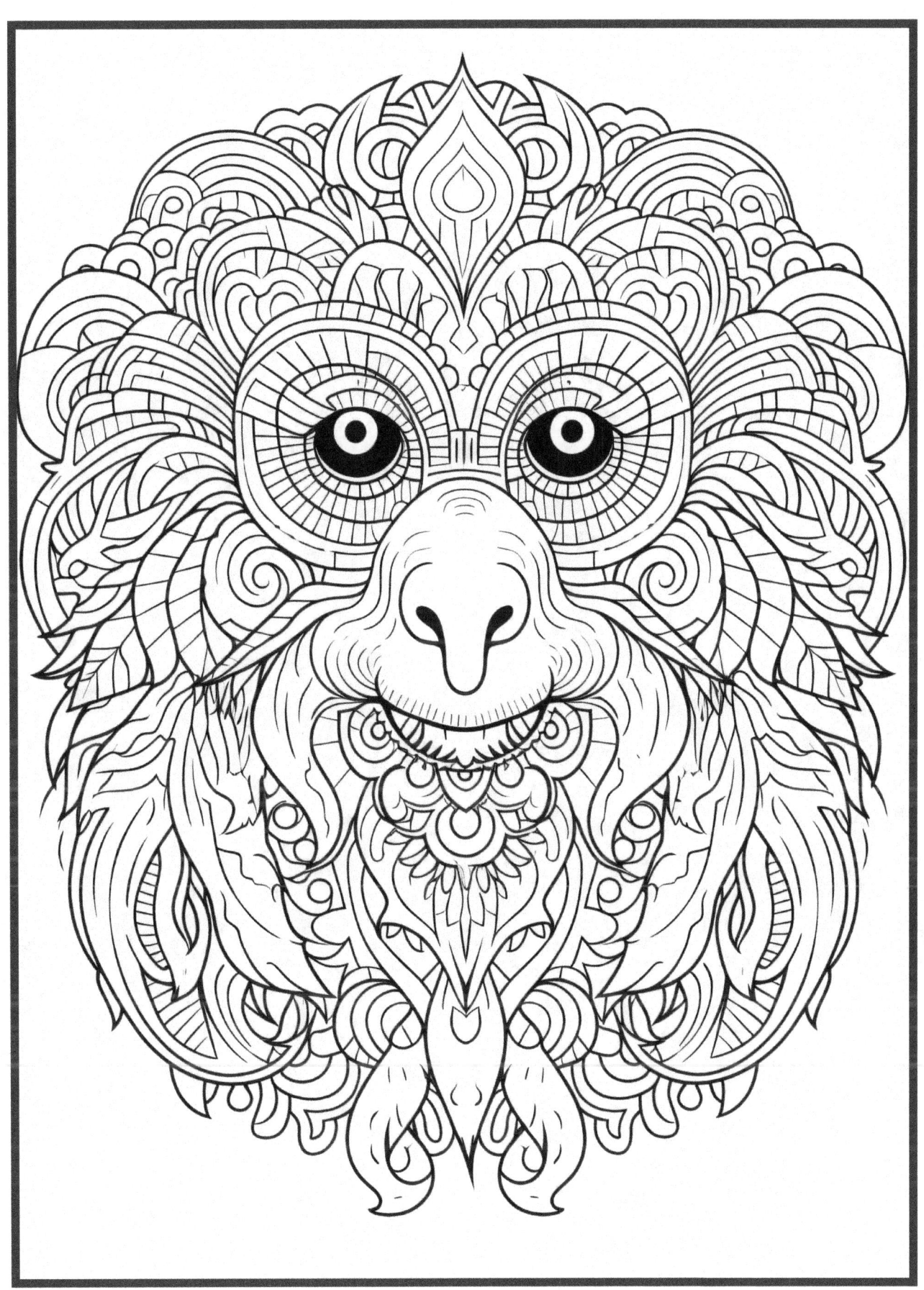

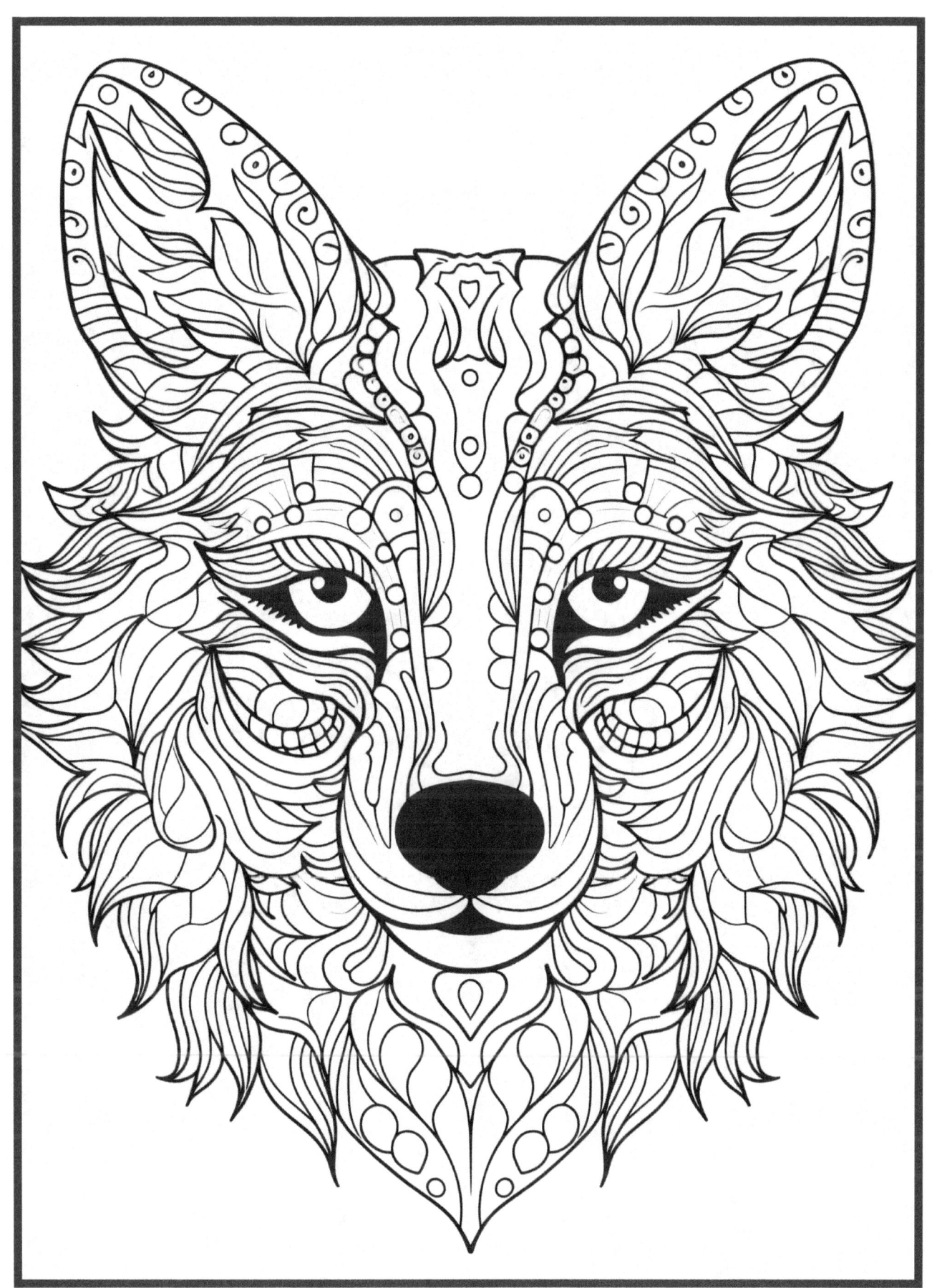

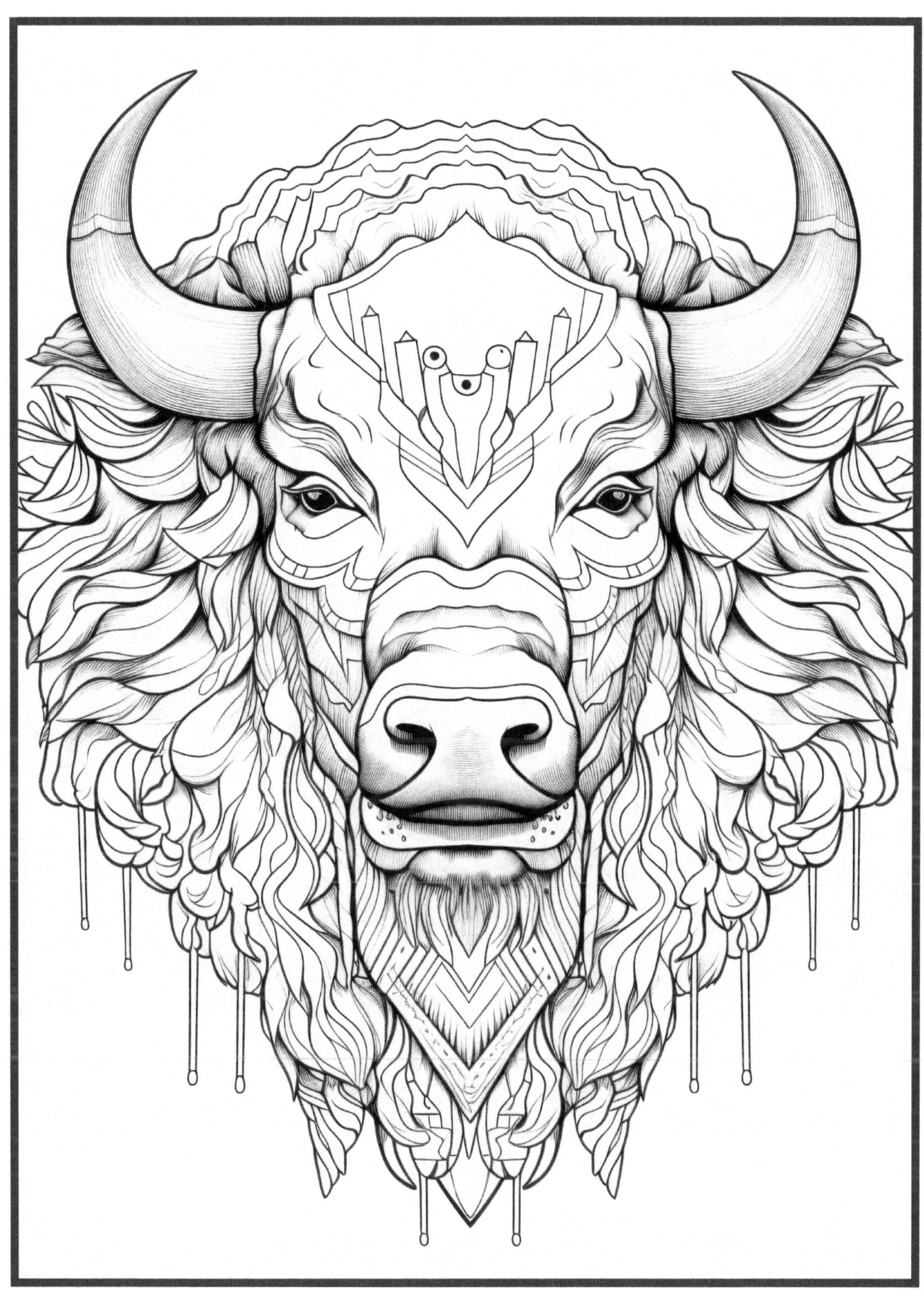

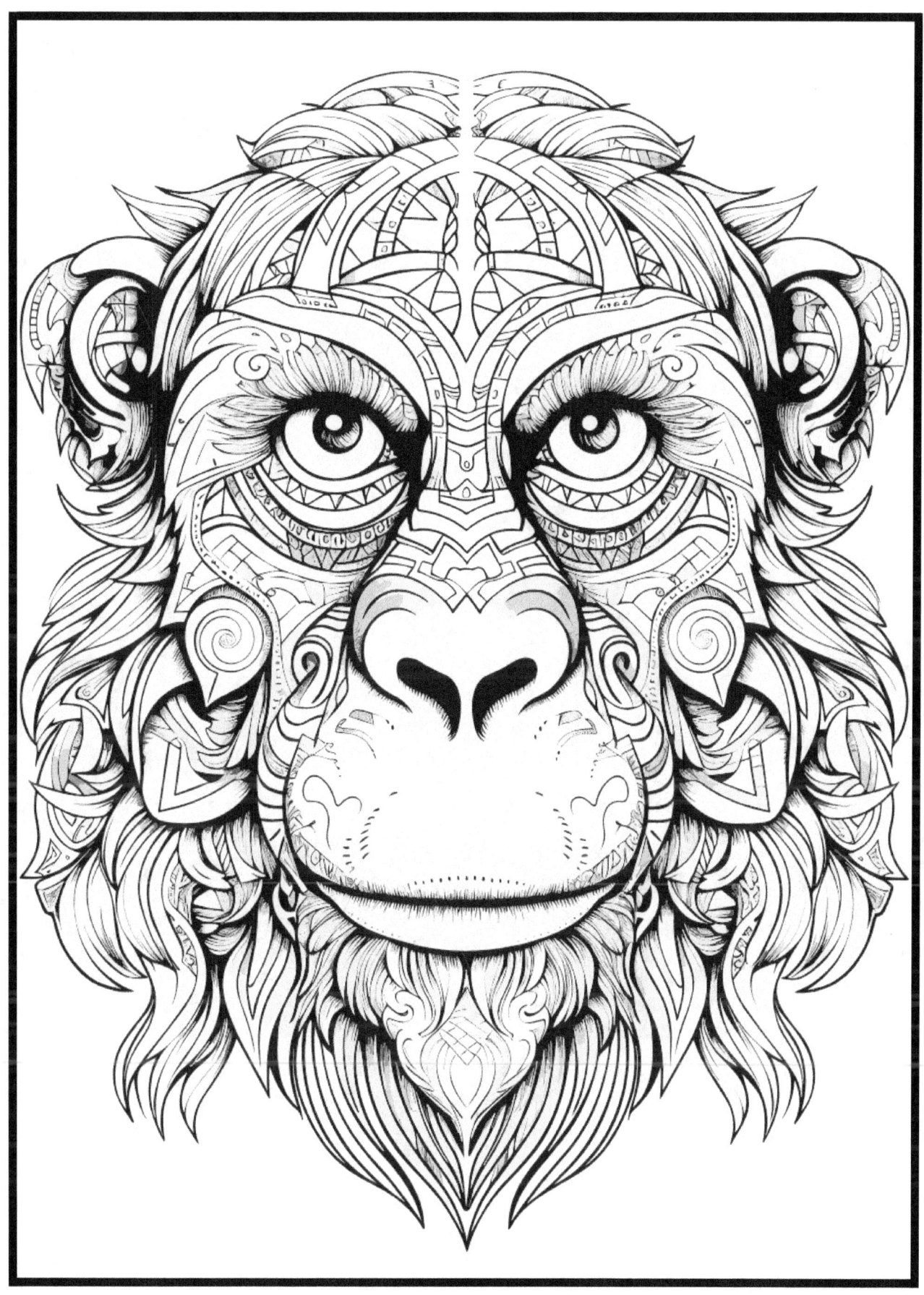

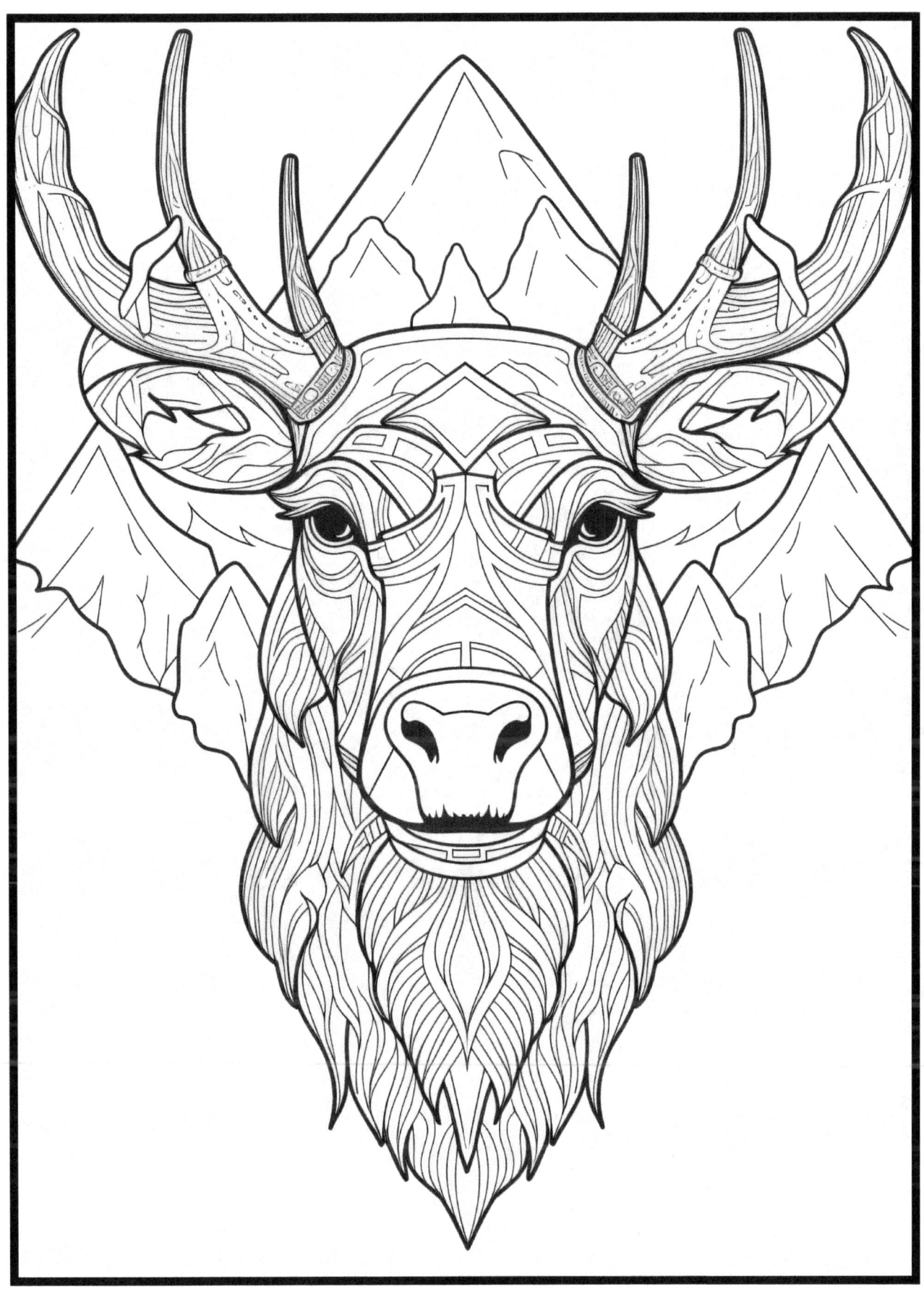

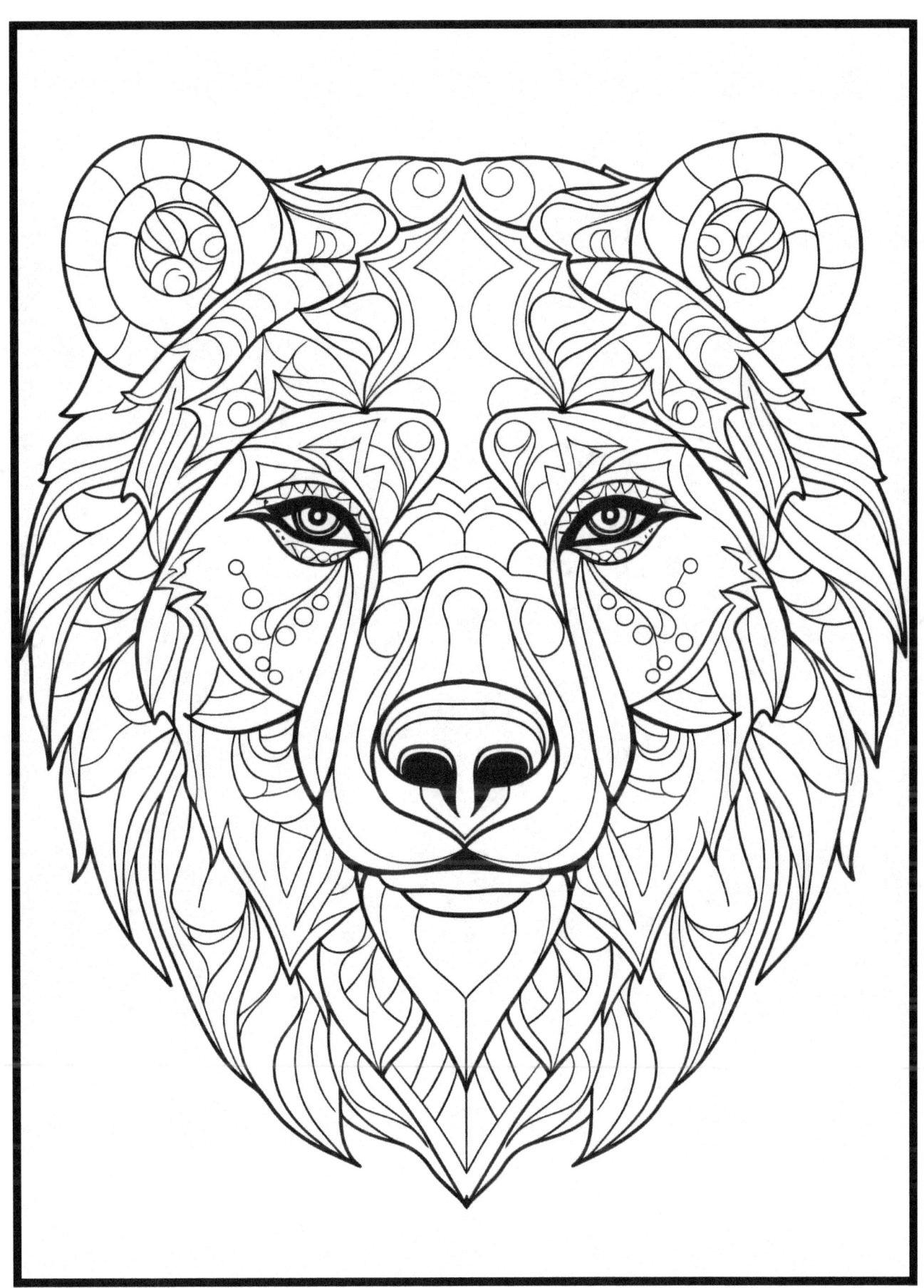

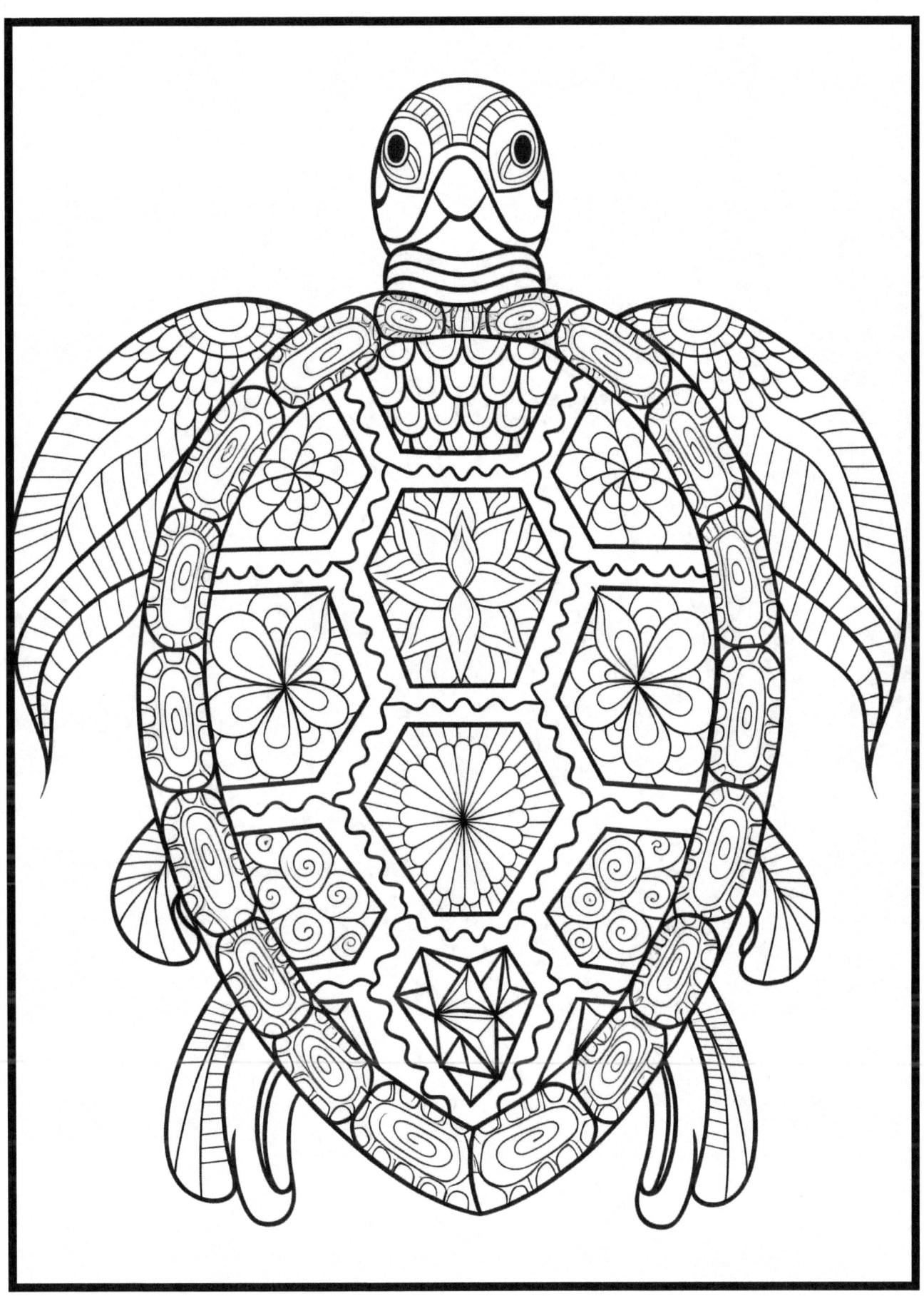

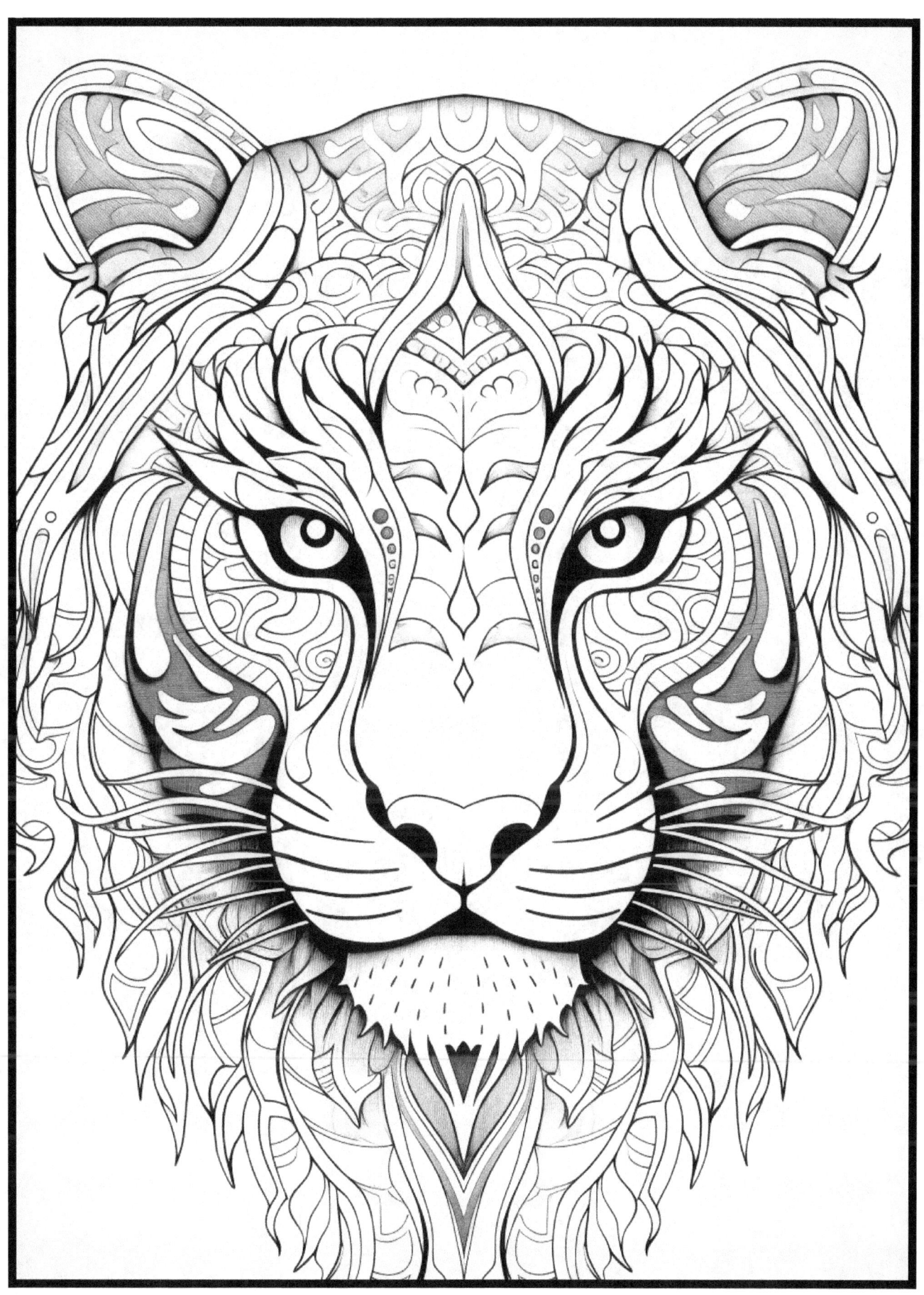

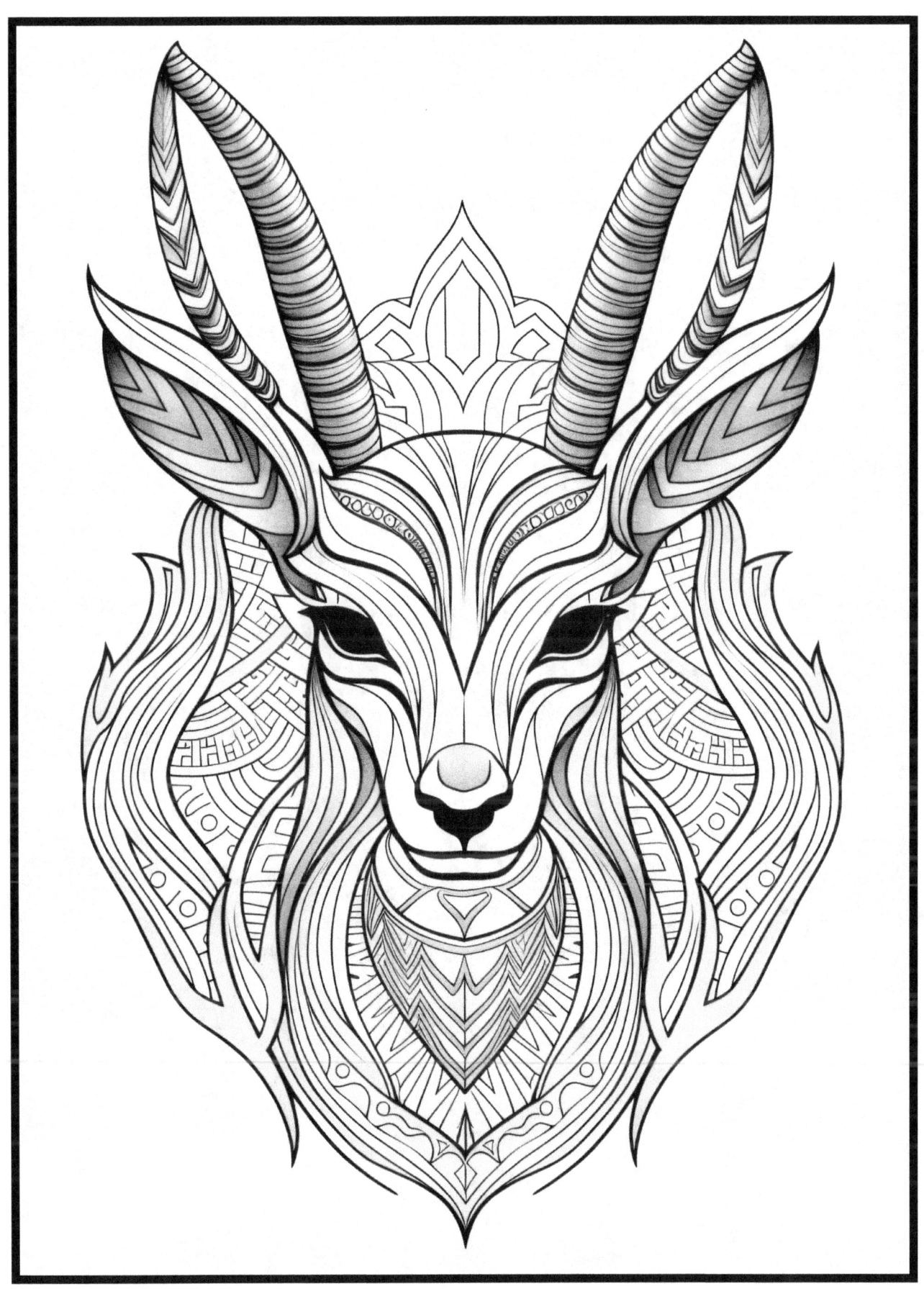

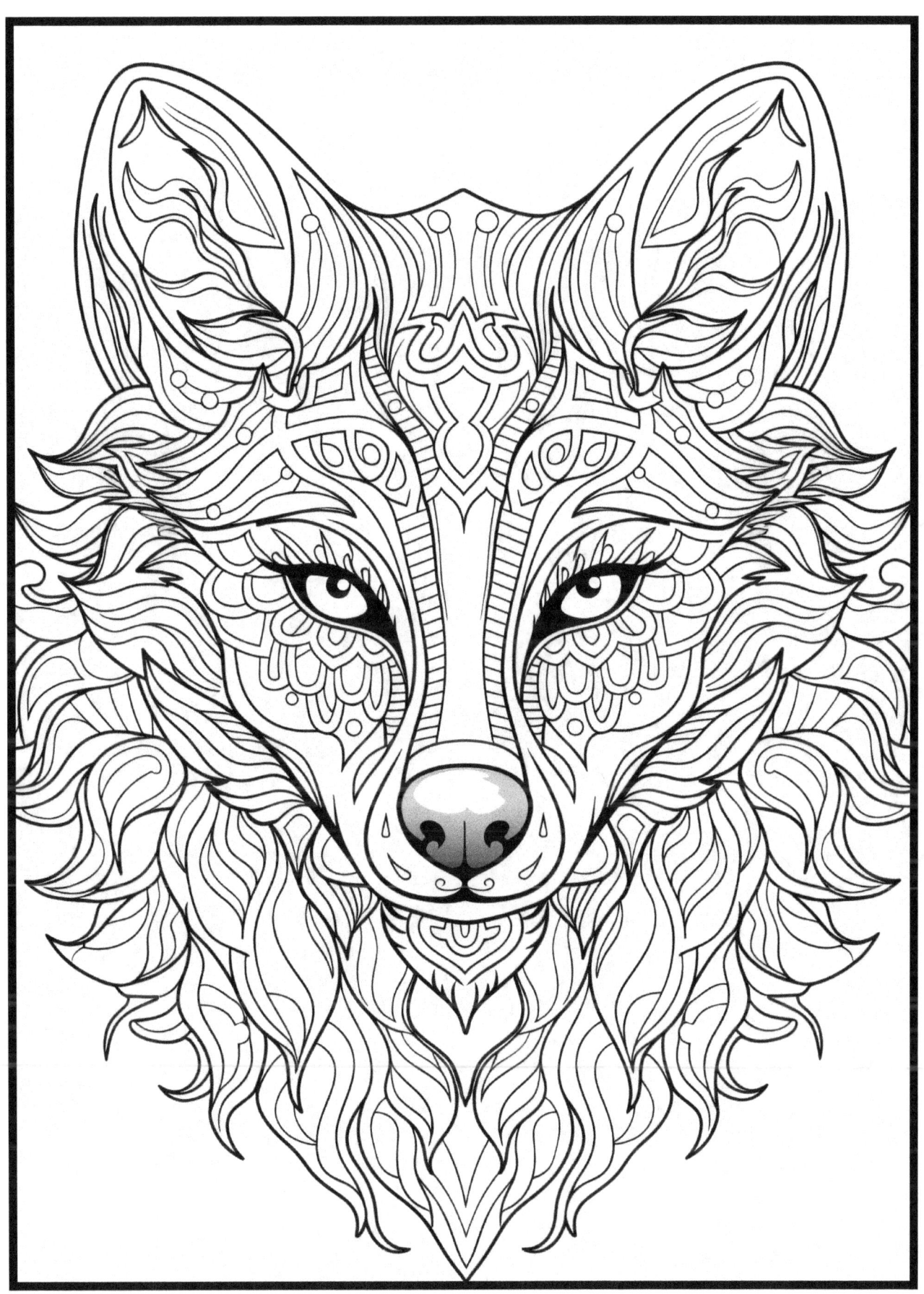

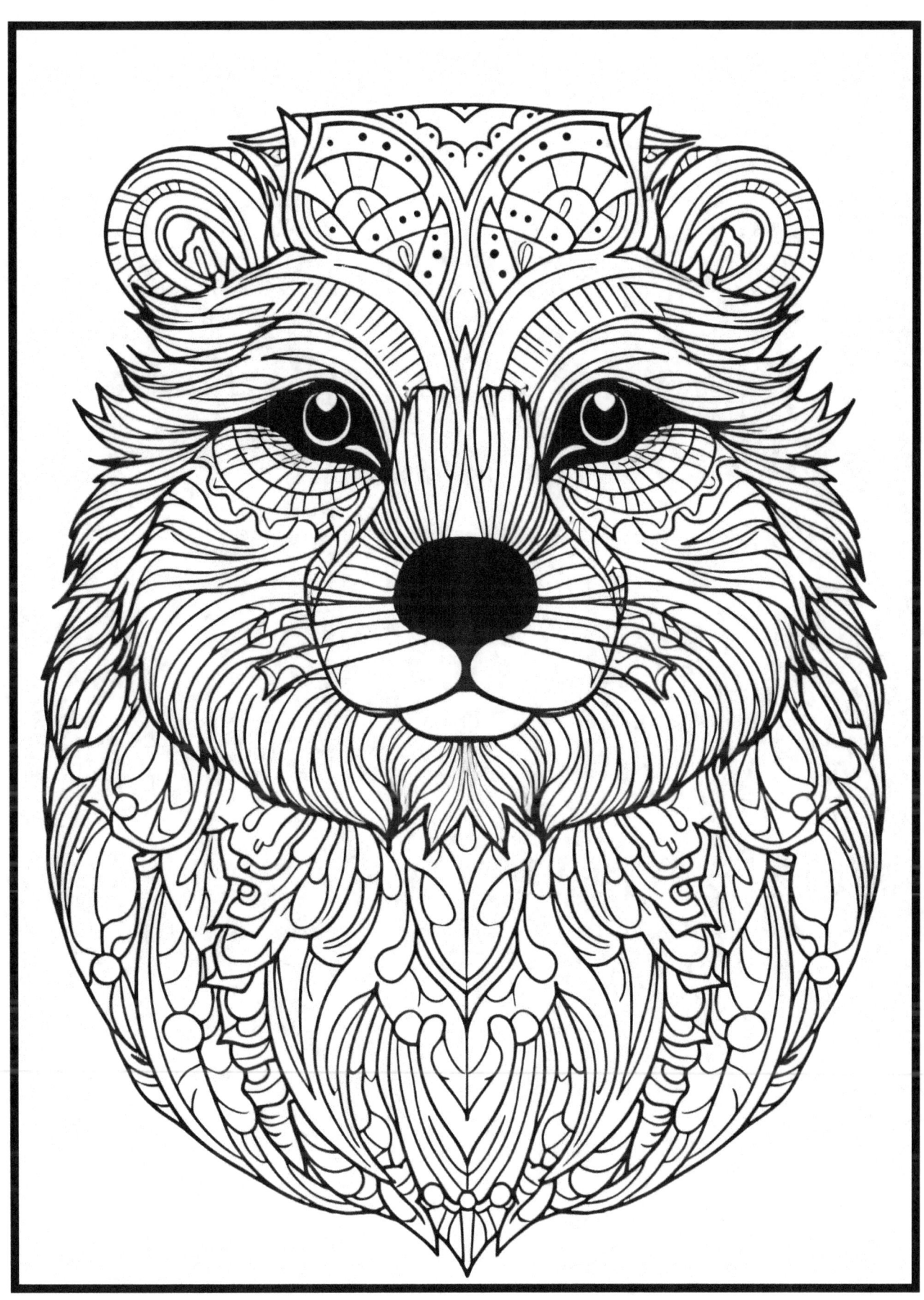